SOCCER PERFORMANCE UNLEASHED

How to Become the Complete Soccer Player

by Bruno Luis

Co-Authors: Craig Simpkin & Shea Robinson

Published by Bruno Luis
ISBN: 978-0-9935404-3-1

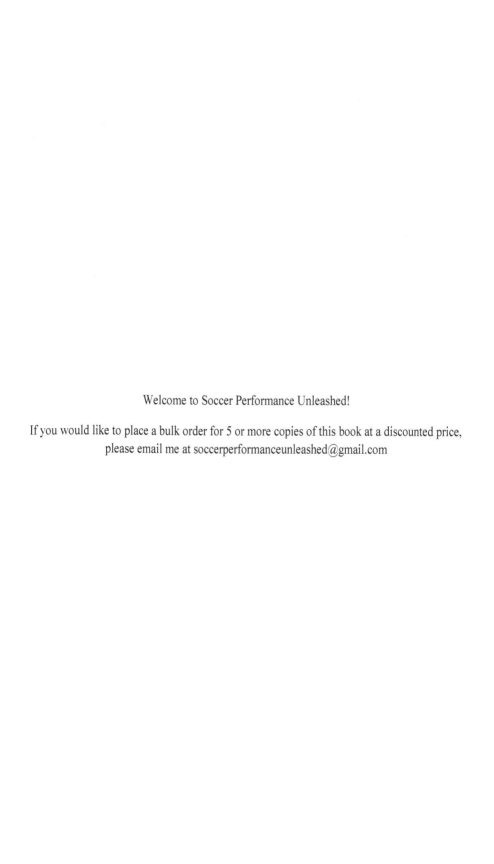

Welcome to Soccer Performance Unleashed!

If you would like to place a bulk order for 5 or more copies of this book at a discounted price, please email me at soccerperformanceunleashed@gmail.com

Table of Contents

Introduction

Do you dream of improving your performances out on the soccer field, but aren't sure where to start? Whether a complete newcomer or a more seasoned player, we can all benefit from taking the time to study in greater detail to improve not only our ability but also our understanding of this often complex sport.

This book will guide you through many of the key aspects of soccer and help you improve your overall game. It will go through the many technical aspects that will improve your game when it comes to striking and controlling the ball, and also ensure that you are completely prepared to play the tactical side of the game with insights in both team and position specific tactics.

Not only that, you will also receive key information regarding the psychological, physiological and off-the-field parts of the game – diet, mindset, fitness, etc - that will enable you to make the most of your talent. The upshot of all of this is that you will arm yourself with all of the knowledge you will need to maximise your potential.

As well as knowledge, another important concept that will help you in becoming the best player you can be is practise. Knowledge and practise are key! Both are needed to make improvements in your soccer ability; and while practise is easy to come by (as a minimum all you need is a ball), the knowledge you need to improve your game can be much harder to obtain.

The ultimate aim of this book is to supply you with the knowledge of how to improve your soccer ability, but the rest will be up to you. Practise, practise, practise!

To achieve the level of performance you want to achieve, not only do you need to practise hard, but you need to practise smart as well. What I mean by this is by gaining a deeper understanding of what you do on the training field and how it affects your skill set can make your training much more effective.

To help you practise smarter, on chapter 11 you will find a fun and interactive way of figuring out your own level of skill and performance. It's a great way to target the soccer attributes you think you need to improve on and how the book will help you in developing that attribute.

I hope you enjoy this book, and that it proves useful to you in your quest to becoming the complete soccer player. Keep it close at all times and continually refer back to the various chapters; you never know, they could make that 5% difference that determines how far you can go in the beautiful game.

Chapter 1

Technique

Great technique is the part of soccer that wows the spectators and makes it such a fascinating sport to watch and compete in. Whether it's a defender performing a perfectly timed challenge, a winger dribbling past opposing players, or an attacker hitting the sweet spot on the ball, technique is the core ingredient of soccer. The greatest players in the world have worked on their technique day-in and day-out to perfect their skills.

Dedication is the key to improving your technique and putting in the time to practise will result in your skills improving. Although there are general techniques such as controlling the ball, passing, and heading which apply to players in every position, there are also certain techniques that must be mastered to become the best you can be in your chosen position. For instance, defenders must learn how to tackle with precision and anticipation, wingers must learn how to dribble with the ball close to their feet, and forwards must be able to strike a ball with power and accuracy.

The key to becoming the best player you can be is mastering the basics and improving your technique from there. It is useless if a defender can tackle with perfect timing but is afraid to head the ball. Or if a midfielder has a world class first touch but struggles to find a teammate with a pass. Or a forward strikes the ball with incredible accuracy but is unable to bring it under control. Practising all of the following techniques are what will make you a top player, rather than simply excelling in one technique and failing in the rest.

1.1 - Controlling the Ball (First Touch)

First things first, controlling the ball. Although ball control and first touch aren't considered the flashiest techniques, they are certainly the most important. Being able to 'trap' the ball instantly using your feet or another body part will give you more time to plan your next move; whether that's to clear the ball if you are a defender, or pick a pass/take a shot/dribble past your opponent in an attack. If your control is inadequate, then you will lose possession of the ball and hand it to the other team. For the very best players in the world, the ball sticks to them like glue – it's almost

an instinctive reaction – and so for yourself developing good ball control is the first building block in becoming a top player.

There are two main kinds of ball control used – wedge and cushion control. Wedge control (also known as touch direction) is when you control and direct the ball in such a way that it pushes it into space and away from an opponent. It involves making contact with the middle of the ball and pushing it in the direction you want to run. This technique is useful to use when you are under severe pressure, or you want to quicken the play.

Cushion control is used when you have slightly more time and can stop or settle the ball at your feet (or any other body part). The most important aspect of this technique is staying on your toes, as it is extremely difficult to adjust your body to the ball if you're flat-footed or stiff. When you're about to control the ball, keep your hips open and face the direction from which the ball is coming. Cushion the ball by moving your foot (or another body part) slightly backwards just before the point of contact with the ball.

Ball Control Techniques

During a match, the ball could come towards you at any height or any speed. Therefore, it is important to be able to control the ball with any part of your body. Each part of the body requires a different technique to maximise control of the ball.

- Inside of the Foot

When using the inside of your foot to control the ball, don't plant the supporting foot flat on the ground. Instead, keep the weight on your toes to help maintain balance. Make contact with the ball using the arch of your foot and cushion the ball by moving your foot along the ball's path.

- Outside of the Foot

If a teammate plays a pass from the side, you may need to use the outside of the foot for control. It is also useful being able to use the outside of your foot if you are running through on goal and don't have time to adjust your body and control the ball with the inside of your foot. As the ball comes towards you, make contact using the area on the bottom outside part of your laces for maximum control.

- Sole of the Foot

Using the sole of your foot for ball control can be the perfect way to get out of a tight spot and create space to run in. When using this technique, place your foot on the ball with your toes slightly raised above your heel. You can then drag the ball back to change direction quickly or move the ball from side to side when dribbling.

- Instep

The instep is mainly used to control the ball when it is falling from a height. The secret to using this technique is to be prepared. Don't simply wait for the ball to arrive, but stay on your toes and be ready to adjust quickly to the ball's trajectory. Try to cushion the ball using the shoelace area on your boot, and at the moment of contact withdraw your controlling foot by slightly bending your knee and ankle.

- Thigh

Another technique that is sometimes used to control the ball when it is falling from a height, the thigh trap can help you gain quick control of the ball during a match. Be sure to position yourself correctly, moving your body according to the trajectory of the ball. Adjust your thigh so that the ball is directed towards the ground. Retract your thigh at the moment of contact so the ball doesn't simply bounce off.

- Chest

The chest is one of the most efficient body parts for control as it provides such a large surface area for both receiving and trapping. When using your chest to control the ball, stretch out your arms and slightly arch your back. Depending on the flight of the ball either bend your knees or jump to align your chest with the height of the ball when receiving.

Ball Control Practise

Improving your ball control and first touch can be achieved with plenty of practice. If you have a training partner, ask them to throw you the ball with varying height and speed. Control the ball with different parts of your body before passing the ball back to them. Take turns in throwing each other the ball and increase the difficulty in the throws as you go.

If you don't have a training partner, you can practise ball control against a wall. Stand between three and five meters away from the wall and kick the ball against it, controlling the ball by trapping or receiving each time it comes back.

Touch Direction

Once you have mastered a good first touch of the ball, your next step should be to improve your touch direction. In tight areas of the field where a number of players gather, such as in midfield, this can be the difference between finding space from which to build an attacking move and being ushered off the ball by a hard-working opponent.

With good touch direction, you can put distance between the ball and your marker, and this will also present you with an opportunity to get your head up and look for that next pass without worrying about your marker stealing the ball from you. So when you receive the ball, think about the angles from which your opponents will try to 'attack' you, and make sure your first touch takes the ball away from this area.

Top Tips:

✓ Practise controlling the ball with both feet instead of just using your preferred foot.

✓ Mix trapping and receiving to improve all-round ball control.

✓ Don't just wait for the ball to arrive, attack the ball as you control it to simulate conditions in a soccer match.

1.2 - Kicking the Ball

Regardless of your position, the technique you use and the understanding you have of your ball kicking technique can set you apart from the rest. Whether you're short passing, long passing, or shooting, you will be reliant on your technique to send the ball where you want it to go.

Knowing which part of the foot to use, or how the ball reacts when struck in a particular place, or how your body shape and position affects the way the ball is struck are the first steps in learning and improving your ball kicking technique.

When you kick a ball, there are three fundamentals to the technique. These are:

✓ The part of the foot you use.

✓ The part of the ball you strike and how much power you use.

✓ Your body shape and position when striking the ball.

Learning these fundamentals and how they affect the ball will allow you to perfect your ball kicking technique:

(As you go through this book you might want to refer back to these three fundamentals)

1. Using your Foot

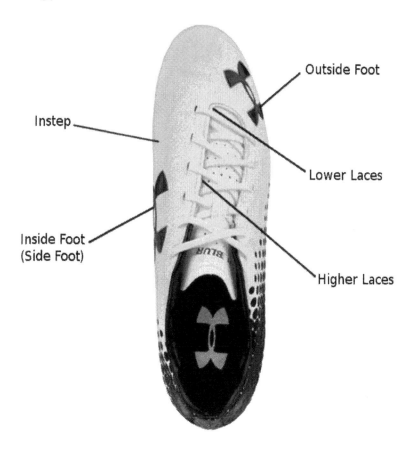

Outside Foot

Instep

Lower Laces

Inside Foot
(Side Foot)

Higher Laces

* Diagram of a right foot

- Instep

The instep is one of the most widely-used parts of the foot in soccer. From here, you can achieve a great amount of power, loft and swerve, which is why many players these days use the instep for striking dead balls like corners and free kicks, and when shooting from distance. The instep provides the perfect balance between power and precision, and striking the ball cleanly with it should be one of your first training methods for improving your game.

- Inside Foot (Side Foot)

The inside of your foot (or the side foot as it's often known) is an area from which you will gain the most control when striking the football. You will not be able to achieve much if any loft or power from your instep, so this is the part of the foot commonly used for simple passes along the ground and when trying to beat the goalkeeper in a one-on-one situation.

- Outside Foot

Striking the ball well with the outside of your foot is a difficult skill to master, but if you put the hours in on the training ground, then you will find that you have access to a unique skill that affords you plenty more options out on the field. Many players will use the outside of their stronger foot instead of their weaker foot to replicate such movement of the ball, and using the outside of the foot is a great way to impact plenty of swerve on the ball. A clean strike will generate plenty of power and cause the ball to dip and curl in the air.

- Lower Laces

The lower laces are one of the most powerful regions of the foot, and with a good backlift and follow-through, you can generate some awesome power on your shots and passes. By striking the ball with the lower part of your foot, you can get right underneath and create plenty of loft. Should you find yourself in the position to need to chip the opposition goalkeeper, use your lower laces to get the ball 'up and over' them.

- Higher Laces

You should only really use your higher laces when the ball comes to you on the half volley or normal volley. This is because you will be able to achieve more control over your strike of the ball, but still create enough power that you can trouble the goalkeeper with your shot or propel your pass to a teammate stood a good distance away.

2. Striking the Ball

The diagram on the left represents the **height and power** of a ball when it is struck in a particular place. The darkest part of the shade (just below the center of the ball) is the optimum place to strike the ball for maximum power and good height. Striking just above the center of the diamond will ensure the ball is hit low, but it will be more difficult to hit it at maximum power. Striking under the center of the diamond will cause the ball to go higher. The higher you want the ball to go, the more power you might need to sacrifice.

This diagram represents the **curve and power** of a ball when it is struck in a particular place. The darker the shade of the ball, the more power you can use to strike the ball. The lighter the shade, the more curve you can put on the ball. As you can see the more curve you want to put on the ball the less power you will be able to use, and vice-versa. More advanced players are able to create topspin or backspin on the ball.

3. Body Shape and Position when Striking the Ball

Your posture when striking the ball is indicative of how accurate and how far the ball will travel. By leaning back (within reason – you shouldn't be able to do the limbo in this position!), you are able to create different angles that generate more power and also the ability to kick the ball higher and further. By leaning forward with your head over the ball upon impact, you are in far greater control of its final destination, although you won't be able to generate as much power.

Standing foot placement will also help; place your standing foot close to the ball for precision, and further away when you need to generate more power.

Kicking the Ball Practise

Improving your ability to kick the ball in different scenarios can be gained through practise. If you have a training partner, you can both practise by passing the ball back and forth. You can vary the distance between yourself and your partner to improve your range and try different kicking techniques. If you don't have a training partner, you can still practise by kicking a ball against a wall.

The best way to improve your technique is by gaining a full understanding of the cause and effect of how you strike the ball, and by replicating those techniques over and over again.

Top Tips:

✓ Ask your training partner to throw the ball towards you when practising volleys. If you are training alone, throw the ball in the air at different heights to practise volleys.

✓ When practicing, try to spend at least 10 minutes kicking the ball with each technique to improve your overall game.

✓ When receiving the ball, try to control it in different ways to also improve your control.

1.3 - Passing

Passing is the bread and butter of any player. As soccer is a team sport, you must be able to pass the ball to your teammates to keep the game flowing or create goal scoring opportunities. Some of the greatest teams in the world are famous for placing a strong emphasis on team play and sharp passing.

There are different ways to pass the ball including short and sharp passing, long and accurate passing, and through balls. The style of passing used by a team is usually down to the tactics employed by the coach, but as a player, you must be capable of picking out the right pass when the opportunity arises.

Short Passing

Short passing is a skill that every player on the field must possess. It can be used to work through an opposition's defense or maintain possession for an extended period during a match. When making short passes, players rely on accuracy over power as the aim is to find a teammate without surrendering possession.

• Side Foot Pass

Also known as the push pass, the side foot pass is the most reliable and accurate way of passing a ball over short distances. Regardless of your position on the field, every player must be able to play side foot passes regularly throughout a match. The technique for a side foot pass includes:

1. Angle of Approach. Make sure you approach the ball at the correct angle in relation to where you want to play the pass. The typical angle of approach is directly facing the intended target.

2. Placement of Standing Foot. The standing foot should be around 5-7 inches from the ball to the side, facing in the direction of the intended target.

3. Placement of Body Weight. All of your body weight should be carried on the standing foot for perfect balance.

4. Position of Striking Foot. The striking foot should be at an angle of 90 degrees with the ankle and foot locked in place. The knee should be bent so that the lower part of the leg creates as large a surface area as possible.

5. Striking the Ball. The striking leg should be swung towards the ball, hitting it in the center with the instep of the foot. As you make contact, keep your head down to ensure the ball glides across the grass.

6. Follow Through. Keeping your weight on the standing foot, follow through the ball for perfect accuracy.

The best way of practising the side foot pass is to use a training partner or a wall and pass the ball back and forth. Only use the side of your foot when passing and controlling the ball to become more comfortable using the instep of your foot. Use both feet when practising and as you improve, try passing the ball using the side foot pass without controlling it first. Doing this will improve your ability to make a first time pass, which you will most likely need to perform in a match.

- Wall Pass

A variation of short passing which you will often see performed is the wall pass or the one-two pass. A wall pass is performed when a player plays a short pass to their teammate and then receives a pass back very quickly from the same teammate. This type of passing can be extremely effective when trying to create space, beat a defender, or get through on goal. The technique for a wall pass includes:

1. Angles. The angle created is the most important part of a wall pass. Typically the angle will be around 45 degrees for the first pass and another 45 degrees for the second pass. These angles are what create the space to beat defenders and hopefully open up a goal scoring opportunity.

2. Accuracy and Power. Both passes in a wall pass must be extremely accurate and played with enough power to reach their intended target. The first pass must have enough pace to make it easy for the receiving player to rebound the ball back to the original player in space. If the ball is hit without sufficient accuracy or power, the wall pass will fail.

3. Creating Space. As the first pass is played, the receiving player needs to recognise where the ball needs to be played. To do this, the original player must immediately create the

desired space for the return pass. A common mistake is to run immediately into the desired space, bringing a defender along. However, a perfectly timed run will open up much more space from the second pass.

4. Communication. As soon as the first pass is played, the original player should indicate where they want the return pass to be made. This can be done by shouting, eye-contact or pointing to the position where you want the ball played.

Practising a wall pass takes a lot of time as it involves a number of attributes that are all required in a split second. The best way to improve is to practise the side foot pass with a training partner or against a wall until you feel confident in your ability. Then, practise with one or several teammates playing sharp and quick passes to one another. You can even have someone trying to get the ball from you to simulate a real match.

Long Passing

Long passes can be used to split open defenses, relieve pressure, and switch possession from one flank to the other. Mainly used by defenders and midfielders, it requires pinpoint accuracy, a high level of leg strength, and the ability to read the game and see where a pass can be made.

- Driven Pass

The driven pass uses a combination of technique and power to hit a ball long distances with pace and accuracy. It is generally used if there are no players or obstacles in between the passer and the receiver and is the quickest way to get the ball from A to B.

A driven pass can be effective when switching play from one side of the field to the other or when playing a ball from defense or midfield to a player further up the field. The techniques for a driven pass include:

1. Once you have selected your target, keep your head down.

2. Plant your supporting foot beside the ball, facing in the direction of the intended target.

3. Keep the striking leg and foot flexed throughout the movement.

4. Strike the ball in the center with the laces of your boot.

5. Point your toes towards the ground when striking the ball.

6. Follow through.

To practise and improve your driven pass technique, set up cones at varying points around a field. Have a training partner pass you the ball at a variety of heights and speeds. Control the ball with one touch and then play a driven pass towards a selected cone. Keep the ball as low as you can, as driven passes are easier to receive when directed at the feet. If you are practising alone, start with your back to the cone, quickly turn and hit the driven pass.

- Lofted Pass

A lofted pass is another type of long passing which you will often see executed in a match. It is played when a player wants to pass to a teammate over opposing defenders and is used to switch the play and change the angle of attack.

Accuracy is more important than power when playing a lofted pass as you are seeking out a teammates head or trying to weight the pass for a teammate to run on to. The techniques used in a lofted pass include:

1. Perfecting the ability to hit a lifted pass from a variety of angles. The pass may be hit from outside the box or on the byline, so it is important to have your angles right.

2. The standing foot should be placed behind the ball and to the side to achieve a perfect loft.

3. Strike the underside of the ball and lean back slightly so it will rise into the air.

4. Use the top of your foot and not the toe when striking the ball.

5. Follow through, keeping your weight on your standing leg.

To practise your ability to make a lofted pass, you can use a cone or a training partner. If using a training partner, stand varying distances from each other and pass the ball back and forth while trying to achieve the correct loft on the ball.

Alternatively, place a cone on a field and try to hit the cone from different angles and distances with a lofted pass. The best way to practise is to constantly change the angle and swing to recreate positions you may find yourself in during a match.

Through Balls

One of the most spectacular and exciting forms of passing is the through ball. It's is a pass that is played between the opposition's defensive line for a teammate to run on to and hopefully get a one-on-one opportunity with the goalkeeper.

Through balls have huge variation and can be long driven passes or short passes such as the wall pass. They can also be played as a straight pass or at an angle depending on the run of the player you are aiming for. Midfielders are usually the players who will excel at this skill, creating excellent goal scoring opportunities for their team. The techniques involved for through balls include:

1. The Angle of the Pass. Choosing the correct angle for a through ball is what makes it work. If you play the ball in between the opposition's defenders at the correct angle, you give your teammate the best chance of collecting the ball and creating a one-on-one opportunity.

2. The Strength/Pace/Weight of the Pass. This is the most difficult part of playing a through ball. Not only must you judge the pace of the defenders you are trying to play the ball in between, but also the pace of the receiving player and the condition of the playing surface. Play the ball too quickly or softly and the defenders will get there first, strike the ball too strongly, and it will go straight to the goalkeeper, play it too late and the receiving player will be offside.

3. Height of the Pass. In a split second you will need to decide what height you want to play the through ball at and adjust your body accordingly.

To become a master of through balls, you must possess the ability to play every single variation of short and long passes. Through balls require the ability to quickly judge which type of pass is the best to play and, therefore, requires a high level of skill in all variations of passing.

Master your Passing

It doesn't matter which position you play: passing is a key art form that you are going to need to master if you are to fulfil your potential. It is the basic building block that maneuvers the ball around the field in the most economical and effective fashion, and as such you will be expected to play your part in this.

Remember to keep your head up as much as you can when in possession and before receiving the ball. This will give you a picture in your mind of how much time you have on the ball and also which of your teammates are in space to receive the next pass from you.

By having this 'map' in your mind, you can treat soccer like a game of chess: enabling you to stay one step ahead of the opposition. If you know that you will be put under pressure by an opponent, you can look to take fewer touches of the ball before releasing it again, or better still, pass it to a teammate first time. If you know you are in good amount of space, then you can get your head up and take your time picking your next pass.

Top Tips:

✓ Remember to deliver the ball to your teammates as you would like the ball passed to you.

✓ Keep in mind how the receiver would best control the ball. E.g. can the receiver control the ball comfortably with either foot or just the one in particular.

1.4 - Dribbling

Sometimes, when an easy pass isn't available, or you find yourself isolated one-on-one with an opponent, attempting to dribble the ball past the opposition can be the gateway to creating a goalscoring opportunity. Other times you might be lucky enough to find yourself in so much space that you can move forward with the ball at your feet. Naturally, the basic tenet of good dribbling is to keep the ball as close to your feet as possible, so that an opponent cannot put it a tackle.

The easiest way to do this is with short taps of the ball with either the instep or toes of your predominant foot, using your peripheral vision to keep one eye on the ball and the other planning your next move. If you have more space to accelerate into, then you can keep your head higher up to look for a pass and allow the ball to get slightly away from you but still close enough that you are in full control.

Shielding the Ball

One of the first technique's a player should learn is how to protect the ball. Time and time again you will find yourself under pressure from an opponent with nowhere to play the ball. In this situation you need to be able to shield the ball so that you don't lose possession for your team.

The key to shielding the ball is to keep the defender as far away from the ball as you can while still maintaining control of it. To execute this technique correctly, position your body sideways between the ball and the defender. Keep your knees slightly bent to maintain balance, and slightly lean into the defender.

Control and maneuver the ball using the instep, outside and sole of your foot that is farthest away from the defender. Use your arm to keep the defender further away and to feel where they are, but do not grab them as you might give away a foul. If you feel the defender trying to sneak to your left or right now is your chance to swivel away from them in the opposite direction.

When shielding the ball it is natural to keep your head down as your full concentration is going into not giving the ball away, but from time to time look up to see if any teammates are available for a pass.

Dribbling at Speed

By using only the very extremes of your feet to maneuver the ball, you will find yourself being able to dribble at a faster speed than if you engage the whole of your side foot or laces in pushing the ball in the direction you want to travel. One of the key aspects of dribbling is to maintain your balance at all times. Otherwise, you could trip over the ball (not cool) or be easily brushed off it by an opponent. So keep shifting your body weight to keep a strong center of gravity.

Perhaps the hardest part of dribbling at pace is maintaining control of the ball while keeping your head up to monitor the positions of your teammates and the opposition. This is not an easy skill to master and does take time and practise. You need to work on keeping the lower third of your vision on the ball, and the rest on scoping out the situation on the field.

Stride Length

Having a short stride length is important if you want to maximize your dribbling ability. A short stride length simply means decreasing each step length (taking more steps as you run) and increasing step frequency (move your legs faster). Although this might compromise your maximum speed, it will improve your acceleration and ball control by allowing you to take more touches of the ball while dribbling.

Some players naturally have a shorter stride length, while most do not. If you're of the latter, then decreasing your stride length means completely changing your running style, so a lot of practice and determination is needed on the training ground. It is also worth noting that if your game is not about dribbling at speed or trying to get past defenders, then changing to a short stride length is not necessary. However, if you're a player whose whole game is about flair and mazy dribbles through the heart of a defense, then changing to a shorter stride length can do wonders for your game.

A perfect example of a player with a short stride length is Lionel Messi. Watch some YouTube videos of him and take notice of his step length while running, his step speed, and how many touches he takes of the ball while dribbling.

Beating an Opponent

It's a tough ask at times, but you may need to outwit your marker at times by dribbling the ball around them. Some of the greatest players ever to grace the field have had an almost unnatural ability to weave their way in and out of defenders; but it really isn't a natural skill, they will have worked tirelessly on the training field to get to those levels.

The general instance in play when trying to dribble past an opponent is a factor is when a winger receives the ball in a wide area and is confronted by a fullback. Now they have two choices to get past them: knock the ball into space and sprint after it if they are quick, or use a piece of skill to work their way around their marker.

A change in pace or direction is perhaps the simplest way to beat a defender. Generally speaking, you will be facing up the field towards your opponents' goal. They will be facing towards you with their backs to their goal. By knocking the ball past the defender when they don't expect it, you will have a small headstart and the advantage of facing in the right direction. They will need to turn quickly in order to beat you in the race, but if you are quick enough and strong enough (they may try to knock you out of your stride using their upper body) then you should get to the ball first.

Beating your opponent with a piece of skill is a lot trickier to define in mere words: you will need to use your instinct to detect a weakness that you can exploit. A classic technique is the body swerve/dropped shoulder, where you feint to move in one direction by opening up your body. This will cause your marker to shift their weight in a specific direction, and you will then be able to dribble past them the other way. Don't worry; it's not as difficult as it sounds, and with plenty of practice you can be a dribbling wizard out on the field!

Top Tips:

✓ Make sure you practise dribbling and shielding with your weaker foot.

✓ Avoid trying to dribble past opponents in your own half. If you lose the ball it might give your opposition a great goalscoring opportunity.

1.5 - Defending and Tackling

The foundation from where a good team can be built is in a solid defense. You may be blessed with brilliant attackers, but if you don't have the ability – as a team – to stop the other team from scoring then you won't win many matches. If you can keep a clean sheet more often than not, then at least you cannot lose the game. Don't forget that a solid defensive performance starts from front to back and so, as a minimum, everybody on the team should know the basics of defending and tackling.

Basics of Defending and Tackling

- Mindset

Strong defending exists beyond just well-timed tackling and good positioning. Taking the right mindset into your role is essential, as this will help you to achieve the right balance between controlled aggression and relaxed, clear thinking. Toughness, timing and technique combine to produce the perfect defense.

Control is the key: if a ball lands in your zone of the field then you will want to make it yours – but not at the expense of being caught out of position or giving a foul away in a dangerous area. By having the mindset that you want it more than your opponent, more often than not you will make that a reality.

- Measure the Distance

Achieving the right balance in defending is also important. Get too close to the player you are marking and they will have an opportunity to spin you or 'give and go'; where the attacker passes the ball to a teammate before running into the space behind. On the other hand, don't get close enough, and you will give the player you are supposed to be marking too much room; and if they manage to score, then it is your fault.

Try to get to within about a meter away from your opponent – this will enable you to halt their progress but retain an advantage should they try to run in behind. If you are up against a quick and skilful opponent, you might need to stand further away. If you're up against a slower and weaker opponent, you should be able to get closer to them.

- Jockeying

To contain or jockey an opponent means to position yourself in front of them and wait until they release the ball far enough for you to intercept it or to tackle. This is the most common technique used by defenders as simply rushing into a tackle will make it much easier for an opponent to beat you.

When jockeying, create a low center of gravity and be on the balls of your feet; ready to move in any direction. Always watch the ball and try not to lunge in, but instead be prepared to backpedal or shuffle sideways if the opponent moves. Don't face the opponent straight on, because this will allow them to simply run past you. Keep at a 45-degree angle forcing your opponent away from goal and remember to stay goal side of them (between the opponent and your goal).

- Patience and Timing

'Don't dive in!' is a cry heard from many a coach when an attacker is running with the ball at a defender. What they mean is be patient and don't jump in with a tackle. Wait for an opportunity to win the ball cleanly.

Sometimes that opportunity won't materialise, but what you can do is still block your opponent's route to goal and take the sting out of an attack with clever defending. Attackers can be tricky with the ball at their feet, and if you dive into the tackle, you increase your chances of being deceived by them.

So don't commit to the tackle too early, and instead be patient. Winning the ball cleanly is the ideal objective but even just containing an attack can be a useful job for your team. Wait for the attacker to lose concentration for a moment or let the ball drift too far away from them; this is your chance to strike. Time your tackle well here and you could break up the attack without breaking a sweat! Finding the balance between aggression, determination and timing is key.

- Controlled Aggression

A good tackle can not only win the ball from an opponent, but it can also show them that you are not a player to be messed with. Controlled aggression is a way to put into practise the three key aspects of tackling – technique, timing, toughness – but with added physicality.

An attacker may shy away from calling for the ball if they know that they have a strong opponent marking them. So remember the basics of being patient and waiting for the right time to strike, and when you do, make sure it is a forceful but fair tackle.

Tackling Techniques

There are many components to defending, but perhaps the most important is tackling. This can stop a dangerous attack in its tracks, and prevent a goalscoring opportunity from being created. But a poorly executed tackle can result in an attacker slipping past or – worst of all - a penalty being conceded. There are three ways of making a tackle; these are:

1. Block Tackle

The block tackle is the most basic form of tackling and can be seen in almost every professional soccer match. When performing a block tackle, plant your supporting foot firmly on the ground to keep your balance. As the opponent makes contact with the ball, use the arch of your free foot to block the shot or pass. When this is timed properly, the block tackle will cause the attacker to stumble or lose the ball.

2. Poke Tackle

The poke tackle requires quick reflexes and perfect timing. To perform a poke tackle, balance yourself on your supporting leg while using your other leg to suddenly stab the ball away from your opponent. It is best to use the foot that is closest to the ball when performing this tackle.

3. Slide Tackle

The most spectacular form of tackle, the slide tackle is also the most dangerous. To perform this tackle requires excellent timing and determination. Firstly, make sure you build enough speed to allow yourself to slide across the ground, then make a sliding motion towards the ball. Once in the slide keep your eye only on the ball, extend one of your feet towards the ball to knock it away from your opponent, and use your arms to control your balance and for protection. NEVER slide tackle from behind, go in cleats first, or raise your foot above ground level as all these can cause significant injury to an opponent.

Interceptions

There is more to good defending than simply making tackles and holding a good position. Making a well-timed interception is another excellent way to break down an attack, although intercepting is an art form in itself. If you press the ball too soon or too late, then you may find yourself hopelessly out of position as the opponents bear down on you goal.

So what are the key components of making an interception? First things first, you must be able to read the game well, and predict what the attacker is about to do next. If you can do that, then you can get into a position on the field where you will intercept their pass with ease.

Keeping the play in front of you is important too. As soon as you are running towards your own goal then you are losing sight of the attackers, leaving them free to do as they please. Instead, try to keep the play is in your field of vision, so you can react to situations accordingly.

Stay patient, and be alert to what is going on around you. If you sense an opponent is about to make a run into space, move yourself into a channel between them and the ball. This will give you the best possible chance of making a crucial interception.

Top Tips:

✓ If possible, try to dictate where you want the attacker to go with the ball, not the other way around.

✓ A slide tackle should mostly be used as a last resort.

1.6 - Shooting

It can take a minute to learn, but a lifetime to master. Shooting is the ultimate asset of attacking players, especially strikers, and those that can strike the ball cleanly with supreme accuracy and power will enjoy a far higher scoring ratio than those who cannot. Ultimately, the aim of a shot is to score a goal, and luckily there are plenty of ways to outfox the goalkeeper who will be doing everything in their power to stop your shot from entering the net. From thunderbolts and volleys to sidefoots and chips, the very best have all of these weapons in their arsenal so that if just one chance comes their way in a match, they are ready to put the ball in the back of the net.

Shooting Technique

Developing your shooting technique is sure to result in more accuracy and power in your shots. There are five main techniques used when shooting; the instep shot, the inside curve/placement, the power shot, volley, and chip shot. Of these types of shots there are numerous variations. However, every great goal scorer has mastered these five fundamental techniques.

- The Instep Shot

From the instep, you can generate a decent amount of power while staying in control of your shot, and so it could be considered a good 'all rounder'. Skilled strikers of the ball and those who put in plenty of practice will also be able to add curve to their shots, which is a great way to fire the ball into the corners of the net.

The instep shot is a good skill to have as you will be able to strike a stationary ball with minimum backlift, a lot of pace, and still be able to maintain precision.

- Placement

Imagine a situation when you only have a small section of the goal to aim at when shooting. Perhaps the goalkeeper is on one side of the goal, or there are plenty of bodies in the six-yard area that you need to accurately place the ball through. This is when the side foot placement shot becomes so invaluable.

You can achieve so much more precision by using your side foot to put the ball exactly where you want it to go, and while you might not be able to generate a huge amount of power, sometimes accuracy is all you need to find the back of the net.

- Power shot

When all else fails, the power shot is perhaps the most basic – but in many ways the most effective – way of beating the goalkeeper. Put yourself in their shoes: would you want to stop a leather ball that is travelling towards you like a missile? It goes without saying. Of course, if you are a long way from goal then the power shot will be your best bet to make the keeper's life as awkward as possible. Whilst close, a power shot will also be hard for them to keep out – as long as the direction is good too.

The technique is fairly simple: keep your upper body steady, as this will help you to keep your balance, and place your non-kicking foot slightly behind and to the side of the ball. Address the ball at near top speed if you can, as this in itself will help you to generate power.

Strike the ball with your laces somewhere around the center of the ball, and remember to follow through to maximise velocity. Don't be alarmed if you feel yourself 'taking off' slightly; this is perfectly natural. And remember: a powerful strike of the ball mostly comes from technique and timing, not just by spending hours in the gym working on your leg strength.

- Volley

Volleying the ball is one of the most difficult skills to master in the game – certainly getting the timing right is, anyway. A well-struck volley can lead to a shot of awesome power though, and some of the most spectacular goals in history have come from volleys.

The difficulty comes from judging the pace and trajectory of the ball as it travels towards you, and then getting into a position to strike it towards goal while maintaining your control over the shot. Some players will naturally take a touch to control the ball, either with their foot, knee or chest, but this can take away the element of surprise that the volleyed shot offers.

Once you have got into position to volley the ball, the principles of shooting then apply: you can strike a power volley with your laces, or a more precision volley with your instep or side foot. The aim, as ever, is to hit the target, but as you will find volleying does – like many things in this beautiful game of ours – take a lot of practice to master!

- Chip

Picture the scene: the opposition goalkeeper has raced off their line to clear the ball, but they only manage to fire it straight to you. The net is gaping, but a mass of defenders stands between you and the goal. If only there were some way that you could get the ball up and over the bodies and into the net behind them....well, there is: it's called a chip shot!

There is a very specific skill to chipping the ball, but once you have mastered it, you will find that it helps you in other aspects of the game too, such as passing and crossing to a tall player. You need to address the shot with your standing foot close to the lowest part of the ball, and then deliver a 'stabbing' motion with the lower laces of your boot to the bottom of the ball. This will cause it to elevate, and if you apply enough force upon striking the ball, it should travel a fair distance above head height.

Long Range Shooting

There are two ways of striking a long-range shot: with power or with placement. The power strike is best when the ball falls to you kindly; sometimes it just sits up nicely and begs to be struck. Here you will want to connect with the ball using your laces, keeping your body weight slightly forward and over the ball for better control of the shot. This will help you to achieve a fast and flat trajectory on the ball.

In other instances, a precision strike is of more value; here you will aim for the corners of the goal to make the goalkeeper's job of saving the shot harder. Connect with the ball with your instep (the inside of the foot), as this will give you more control.

Where to Shoot

Let's take a look at some statistics from a recent study of an international top league of where scored goals most often find their way into the back of the net:

- Top Left: 8%

- Top Center: 4%

- Top Right: 5%

- Middle Left: 7%

- Middle Center: 8%

- Middle Right: 6%

- Bottom Left: 22%

- Bottom Center: 21%

- Bottom Right: 19%

Although these statistics don't account for the various situations in which the goals were scored, it is easy to see that more goals go in when hit low. This makes a lot of sense because it is much more difficult for a goalkeeper to get down to the ground quick enough to save a low and powerful shot.

It is also interesting that over two-thirds of the goals were scored in the corner as opposed to down the middle. This shows how important accuracy is when shooting. If you combine the two conclusions, it seems that shooting low into the corners provides the best chance of success and produces the highest number of goals.

Top Tips:

✓ Try to have each shot type in your locker, so that you can react to any situation and shoot accordingly. When the time comes for precision, power or a chip, you will be ready.

✓ As a bare minimum, make sure you hit the target so that you maximise your chances of scoring.

1.7 - Heading

For many people who are starting out playing soccer, heading the ball can be one of the hardest techniques to master. First, you must get over your natural fear of getting hit on the head by a flying object, and then you must learn how to head the ball without getting injured. It is always worth bearing in mind that if you head a ball correctly and attack the ball rather than letting it hit you on the head, it won't hurt.

When heading a ball, you should strike it with the top part of your forehead and keep your eyes open until contact. A common mistake made by young players is they close their eyes when heading the ball, but this just means they can't see where the ball is and could end up injuring themselves or someone else. Regardless of which position you play, heading the ball is a major part of the game and involves specific technique.

How to Win a Header

All around the field aerial battles will be won and lost. Particularly in the respective penalty areas of the field, the heading duel is all important. You would expect that the taller of the two combatants would win the battle every time, and while they do have an obvious advantage, there is nothing to stop those shorter in stature from winning plenty of headers. There are three things that all players need: a good leap, timing and bravery. Put this trio together and you will find yourself winning headers against even the tallest of foe.

First things first: the leap. You will need to possess explosive power in your legs to propel yourself high off the ground. There are plenty of exercises you can carry out to improve your leg strength, such as lunges and burpees. These will give you the spring to get into the air.

Timing your jump is crucial: too early or too late and you will miss the opportunity. Never take your eye off the ball. Once you're up there, you will need to hold off your opponent using your arms, although you must be careful not to use them as a kind of climbing frame as you will be penalised! But a gentle nudge with your upper body to theirs will help to throw them off balance.

Once you have beaten them in the air, you will need to meet the ball with your forehead; no other part of your head will do UNLESS you are looking to deliver a glancing header to a whipped cross, in which case you can use your temple to add further pace to the ball.

Heading Practise

To improve your heading technique, you can simply play keepy-uppy using only your head with a training partner or against a wall. This will help improve your timing and will teach you where the best spot is on your forehead to head the ball. If you are a bit frightened of heading the ball, this can also be a great way to build up your confidence.

Top Tips:

✓ Make sure you keep your eyes open for as long as you can before you head the ball.

✓ Keep your mouth closed as you are making contact with the ball to avoid injury.

✓ When challenging for a jumping header, try not to swing your arms as this can seriously injure another player.

1.8 - Crossing

When you receive the ball in wide areas, your first thought should be to deliver an effective cross into the box, as this is the quickest route to goal for your team. Ultimately, the effectiveness of your cross will be determined by two things: how accurate it is, and how suitable it is for your attackers. These two things work in conjunction, because no matter how accurate your cross is, if you deliver a high ball to a striker with weak jumping and heading abilities, or a whipped cross to someone who's in-box movement isn't very good, then it will be wasted effort.

There are a few different ways to address the ball and deliver it into a dangerous area. The most natural way is with the instep, which enables you to control the direction and depth on the cross, and – crucially – present your teammate with an easier ball to attack.

A power cross delivered with the laces of the boot, whilst a useful weapon if you want to put the ball into a dangerous area quickly, is a more difficult one for your teammate to apply a telling finish or header too.

If you have a particularly tall striker in your team, then 'standing the ball up' is a handy tactic for allowing them maximum opportunity to reach the cross with their head. You can achieve this by stabbing the lower half of the ball with the lower laces; visualise a golfer chipping the ball out of a bunker – it's the same idea.

Creating Space for a Cross

You only need a yard or so of space to be able to deliver a meaningful cross, but sometimes when you have a determined marker this can be hard to find. So refer back to the dribbling chapter of this book for some handy hints of how to create a bit of space for yourself from which to deliver a cross.

When you watch a world class winger in a match, they will utilise the body swerve or a dip of the shoulder to momentarily throw their marker off balance, and this buys them just enough time to get their head up, pick out a teammate and deliver the ball accordingly.

Top Tips:

✓ Always consider how your target would want the ball to be delivered; this informs how you cross the ball.

✓ Utilise low, hard crosses for short and quick players with good finishing, and floated crosses for attackers who are strong in the air.

✓ Create a bit of space for yourself to deliver a cross with a quick feint or body swerve; this could create a brief opening for you to get your head up and deliver the ball.

✓ Practice hitting crosses first time as you may not be able to take a touch during a match.

1.9 - Art of Deception

Expect the unexpected, so the old saying goes. The art of deception in soccer comes from doing the things that your opponent is simply not expecting you to do. It can be a key weapon on the field and can also make all the difference in tight games.

There are generally 6 main areas in which deceiving your opponents can gain you a crucial advantage. These are:

• Movements

Players generally move in straight lines out on the field, and this makes them easier to mark. So by curving your run, making short and sharp movements, and operating in diagonals, will make you harder to pick up, and swapping positions with relevant teammates (e.g. swapping flanks with a fellow winger, or strikers operating on different sides) adds to your mystique! Most teams, particularly at an amateur level, are set up in systems with 'straight lines', i.e. 4-4-2. So you can deceive your opponents by playing in between their lines of defenders, midfielders and strikers.

• First Touch

The key to the first touch is to maneuver the ball into space and away from your opponents, and that should be your fundamental thought. But doing the unexpected is still an option here, and the best way to catch an opponent off guard is to position your foot and body to 'show' your opponent where you plan to maneuver the ball, and when you receive the ball, you instead steer it in another direction. Doing this should give you more space and time on the ball.

• Passing

All through a match, you might be making simple passes to a teammate or trying to dribble past your opponent at every opportunity, so much so that you have become predictable. You may have been instructed to do these tasks, but your opponents are now able to read you like a book. So don't be afraid to try the unexpected: the lofted through ball, the early cross, the killer pass (hoping that a teammate latches on to it). If your opponents are not expecting it, then they are not preparing for it, and the art of passing deception can unlock even the steeliest of defenses.

Another way of fooling your opponents is by disguising your short passes. Much like your first touch deception, just before you pass the ball, position your foot and body (you can use your eyes as well) to 'show' the opposition where you want them to think you are going to pass to, and in the very last second pass the ball to your intended target. This will make it harder for your opponent to intercept the ball.

• Dribbling

Effective dribbling is about deceiving your opponent into losing their balance or diving into the tackle, and so naturally doing the unexpected is the best way to achieve this. If you have attempted the same tricks in each of your first few dribbles in the match, then try something new the next time.

If you are a left-footed player playing on the left flank, you will be expected to try and go around the outside of your marker on your stronger foot. So try cutting inside instead, which will give you the element of surprise. Deception in dribbling will come from avoiding repetition – variety is the spice you need.

- Defending (Including Tackling)

It is perhaps advisable to minimise your unpredictability as a defender, as your colleagues will be relying on you to perform your duties as part of the unit. Even so, you can act in a deceptive way to fool the attacker by avoiding repetition: if you defend in the same manner each and every time, then the attacker will become accustomed to this and start to formulate a plan to take advantage.

Sometimes tackle upon the attacker receiving the ball, other times hold back a few seconds and strike when the attacker is least expecting it. If they don't know how you are going to tackle them, then they won't feel comfortable in possession.

- Shooting

And lastly, shooting: how are the opponents expecting you to shoot? First time, or after taking a few touches to get the ball exactly how you want it? The most deceiving method of shooting is taking the shot early. A 'snapshot', as it is known, can often catch a goalkeeper unawares, and it is always worth testing out their powers of concentration. Shooting with your weaker foot is also an option, as a defender is likely to show you onto your weaker side as they perceive this to be a safer tactic.

Chapter 2

Team Tactics

At all levels of the game, soccer has become a far more tactical sport in modern times. Gone are the days when both teams would set up in a neutral 4-4-2 formation and hoped they outperformed their opponents on the day and picked up the win.

Nowadays, games can be won by the unique and often minute differences in tactics between the two teams. If you get your tactics right, then you can beat even the toughest of opposition. Get them wrong, and you could be on the end of a bit of a drubbing.

Each coach has their own ideas on the best system to play. But often, tactics go beyond the shape that the team is set up in. It is the balance between attack and defense, whether to keep possession or play a more direct style, whether to press high up the field or defend deep....the list goes on.

Tactics can often be so subtle, so deeply entrenched, that they are almost invisible to the naked eye. But if you watch a game at the highest level with your thinking cap on, hopefully you will be able to see where the match will be won or lost.

Your coach will have their own ideas of how they want the team to play, and it is up to you to learn how your role needs to be played tactically. Because as we've mentioned already, you may be an incredibly gifted player but if you don't understand the tactical aspects of your position then you may find yourself at times struggling through a match.

2.1 - A Guide to the Modern Soccer Team

The game has changed almost beyond recognition in the last 20 years, and now each player's position has changed markedly from that of their predecessors. Just look at the modern central midfielder: it's easy to name about four different types of player alone!

So here's a quick rundown of the skills and attributes that each role requires:

Goalkeeper

This is perhaps the only role on the soccer field that hasn't changed in recent years! The keeper's primary aim is to repel the shots of their opponents and so good handling, shot stopping. and reflexes are needed.

A decent amount of upper body strength will help them to shrug off challenges in the air, and being able to read the game well will also enable the keeper to dash off their line at the right time to foil dangerous attacks. Defenders always appreciate a goalkeeper who communicates well and helps to organize the defensive line, and it's a bonus if they are handy with the ball at their feet too.

Key attributes:

- ✓ Handling

- ✓ Reflexes

- ✓ Shot Stopping

- ✓ Communication

- ✓ Reading of the game

Central Defender

There is much more emphasis on defenders being comfortable in possession and distributing the ball these days, whereas in the old days they were selected more readily for their defensive capabilities.

It's important to be versatile too: some forwards you come up against will be built like the proverbial brick outhouse, while some will be small and nippy. So keeping yourself in good shape as a center back is important.

An ability to read the game, anticipate and time tackles are essential, as is a good leap in order to be competitive in aerial duels. And being able to start attacks by passing the ball effectively is very much a bonus in the modern game.

Many center backs are the vocal heart of a team too, acting as the key motivators and communicators. Hopefully, this is something you feel comfortable with.

Key attributes:

- ✓ Strength

✓ Tackling

✓ Reading of the game

✓ Aerial ability

✓ Concentration

✓ Communication

Fullback

These days the role of the fullback is a dual one: primarily you will need to defend well, close down your opponent and prevent him or her from whipping dangerous crosses into the box or cutting inside to shoot.

And once that duty has been fulfilled, you will need to support your team's attacks by providing width and a cutting edge on the flanks, overlapping the winger where possible and delivering crosses of your own into the penalty area.

Consequently, you need to be a good all-rounder and someone who is equally as comfortable in defense as attack. Your fitness levels will need to be exceptional too, in order to get up and down the field for 90 minutes.

Key attributes:

✓ Tackling

✓ Teamwork

✓ Crossing

✓ Stamina

✓ Positioning

Central Midfielder – Holding

The job of the holding midfielder is the ability to break up the opposition's attacks with good reading of the play and well-timed tackles, and being able to tightly mark the opponents' most attacking midfield threat.

Many of the world's leading holding midfielders are stockily-built (but still good athletes) and strong in the tackle, so you might want to hit the gym if this is the role for you. But understanding the game and pre-empting your opponents' next moves are the most crucial aspects. Win the ball back with a well-timed tackle or interception, and pass it simply to a teammate. It sounds so simple when you put it like that!

Key attributes:

- ✓ Tough tackling
- ✓ Work rate
- ✓ Positioning
- ✓ Anticipation
- ✓ Strength

Central Midfielder – Deep Lying Playmaker

The purpose of the deep-lying playmaker is to act as a conductor; everything creative goes through them. They pull the strings by picking up the ball from their defensive colleagues and build attacks from deep. This is the key link between defense and attack.

The deep-lying playmaker needs great vision and a range of passing: both short and long. They need to be able to read the game and spot a teammates run before they've even made it, so 'soccer intelligence' is a must.

Key attributes:

- ✓ Passing range
- ✓ Vision
- ✓ Creativity
- ✓ Reading the game
- ✓ Positioning

Central Midfielder – Box-to-Box

This is a position that is usually required at the lower levels of the game, where coaches will deploy two box-to-box midfielders in their system. As the name suggests, the object of this player is to offer something in both defense and attack; getting back to support their teammates defensively, but also breaking into the penalty area to try and get on the scoresheet too.

The skill that any box-to-box midfielder must possess is great stamina, in order to propel themselves up and down the field for the duration of the match. In addition, being able to break down and outwork the opposition's midfield will also help, as will an eye for goal. A great all-rounder is required.

Key attributes:

- ✓ Stamina

- ✓ Determination

- ✓ Tackling

- ✓ Passing

- ✓ Finishing

Central Attacking Midfielder

Similar in nature to the deep-lying playmaker, however, this advanced role sees the creative maestro getting on the ball in the final third of the field more; creating goal-scoring opportunities for their teammates and hoping to score a couple themselves in the process.

The advanced playmaker needs to be comfortable in possession and in defeating opponents with their dribbling skills. An eye for goal is a bonus, but creating chances is the key to this role, so an ability to make things happen is crucial.

Key attributes:

- ✓ Passing

- ✓ Dribbling

- ✓ Creativity

- ✓ Vision

- ✓ Awareness

Winger – Modern

The modern winger can often play a slightly different role to their predecessors. Usually, they will play on the 'wrong side', e.g. a right-footed player will play on the left and a left-footed player on the right.

These players cut inside on their stronger foot and look to create chances, link-up play or score themselves. It is an intrinsically attacking position, although the winger may be required to track back and support their fullback.

Key attributes:

- ✓ Dribbling
- ✓ Creativity
- ✓ Ball control
- ✓ Shooting
- ✓ Movement

Winger – Orthodox

This is more of a traditional role where a left-footed player on the left and right-footed player on the right will attempt to run at their opponent, beat them with a dribble, a bit of skill or sheer pace, before whipping a cross into the penalty area.

As you'd imagine, these players have speed to burn, good close control, dribbling and a few tricks up their sleeve to beat their marker. An ability to land crosses on a teammate's head or into dangerous areas is a serious bonus.

Key attributes:

- ✓ Pace
- ✓ Dribbling
- ✓ Crossing
- ✓ Stamina
- ✓ Creativity

Striker – Balanced

A 'balanced striker is someone who leads the line with their strength and tight ball control, drops deep to link-up play and runs in behind the defense for the classic striker's goal.

So a versatile forward with plenty of different attributes is required: but the key principle of the balanced striker is to score goals; that is what they are in the team for.

Key attributes:

- ✓ Finishing
- ✓ Composure
- ✓ Movement
- ✓ Ball Control
- ✓ Strength
- ✓ Guile

Striker – Poacher

The poacher is tasked with putting the ball in the back of the net – nothing more, nothing less. In this role, strikers are not expected to play a key part in the build-up of an attack, but a natural eye for goal and finishing prowess are the poacher's weapons.

Key attributes:

- ✓ Finishing
- ✓ Composure
- ✓ Movement
- ✓ Anticipation

Striker – Target Player

The main goal of a target player is to receive the ball and bring other attacking talents into the game, and, of course, score their fair share of goals. These players can sometimes get isolated in attack, and so it is important that the target player is able to control the ball well and have enough strength to hold up the ball until reinforcements arrive.

Key attributes:

- ✓ Strength
- ✓ Heading
- ✓ Finishing
- ✓ Ball control

✓ Determination

2.2 - Formations

Formations represent a strategic plan and placement of players on the field created by the coach or manager with the aim of accomplishing an effective defensive against an opponent's attack, an effect attack on the opponent's defense, and the ability to win and control the ball in the middle of the field. There are many factors at play when deciding which formation is most suited to a squad of players or a starting eleven including:

- The individual skill of the players who will be starting in each position.

- The collective skill of the eleven players who take to the field.

- The physical strengths and weaknesses of the players according to the demands of each position.

- The formation and tactics that are implemented by the opposition.

- The strengths and weaknesses of the opposition.

- Whether a team is expected to win or if they are playing for a draw.

- Whether a team is playing at home or away.

These are the most common factors in deciding a formation, although there are other circumstances that can determine the coach's decision such as the weather, events that occur during a game (player getting sent off for either side, injury to star player, etc.), and many others.

The evolution of soccer over the last 100 years, and particularly over the last 20 years, has led to a huge range of formations coming into play throughout the professional leagues, with an emphasis on fewer out-and-out forwards and a more equal spacing of players on the field. This means that players today need to have a better all-round game, leading to a reduction of players who are specialists in just one position.

Due to the fluid nature of play, many formations aren't rigid and can be altered and changed during a game, as can player positions. For example, if a coach is playing a 4-4-2 formation it doesn't necessarily mean that players are stuck in their positions and can't move around to help out in other parts of the field.

Within each formation are a host of player roles that can impact how fluid or rigid the formation is during play. These can include designating one player as a playmaker who dictates the play and controls the tempo of the match, or playing a tall target player up front who can hold the ball and get onto the end of crosses from the wide players.

Due to the mathematical possibilities, coaches can produce countless new ways to play the game and set up their side. However, one of the drawbacks of this is players can often get confused on what their role is when a new formation is implemented. But the good news is nowadays a coach is likely to play one of four formations (or a variation of one), these are 4-4-2, 4-2-3-1, 4-5-1, or 3-5-2.

4-4-2

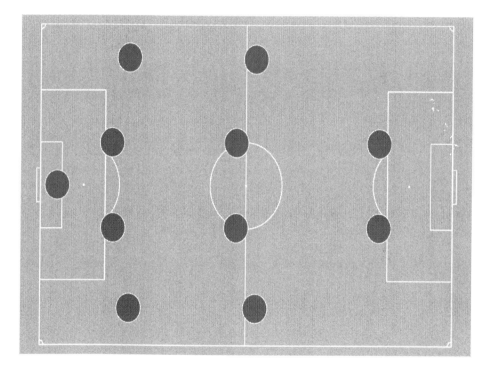

The 4-4-2 formation remains among the most common formations, especially in the amateur leagues, as it is so adaptable and provides a team with plenty of midfield strength and width.

The role of the central midfielders and fullbacks, in particular, can change depending on whether the emphasis is on attacking or defending, with fullbacks afforded more freedom to push forward and provide support to the wingers in this system today than in years gone by. It is also easy for a coach or manager to alter and adapt a 4-4-2 formation depending on how the game is going.

- *Defensive Line*

The formation's back line is similar to the back line of many other formations that use a flat back four. It consists of two central defenders, who generally sit deep and are completely devoted to defending with no intention of getting forward, except during set-pieces. The central defenders can mark a space in a central area (zonal marking), or pick up a designated player (man marking) while their main job is to tackle opposing players and head the ball away from the danger zone. They generally keep the play simple when they have the ball at their feet and look to play short passes to the midfield when moving the ball forward.

Either side of the central defenders are the fullbacks who are responsible for defending the area wide of the central defenders. The primary aim of the fullbacks is to defend against the opposition's wingers and any other players who drift wide on the field and into their territory. However, many fullbacks today often have another role as a support player for their wingers, roaming forward when in possession and offering an option for a pass into space or crossing the ball into the opposition's penalty box.

- *Midfielders*

The two central midfielders in a 4-4-2 formation can be tasked with a variety of roles. In some versions of a 4-4-2 they may be asked to play as a box-to-box midfielder, with their job ranging from shielding and defending in front of the central defenders, to getting forward on the attack to provide late runs into the penalty area. It is also possible to play one defensive midfielder and one attacking midfielder, leaving the defensive duties to one and the attacking responsibilities to the other. Many teams that use this formation will have one central midfielder who specializes in passing and one who is a more physical ball-winning midfielder.

On either side of the central midfielders are the wingers, both of whom have the attacking objectives of providing width and creating goal scoring opportunities. A traditional winger will attempt to beat the defender before crossing into the box for the strikers and central midfielders, but nowadays wingers are also expected to track back and help out defensively. This is especially important when defending against a team that has an attack-minded fullback, so as not to let them double up on your own fullback.

- *Forwards*

Unlike many modern formations that rely on a sole forward, the 4-4-2 has two forwards leading the line and is often built on a great relationship and understanding between them both. There are several ways to deploy the two forwards in this formation, with one of the most common being to play one forward high up the field whose job it is to hold the ball up and lay it off to their partner who plays a little deeper.

The forward playing high up the field is known as a target player and is generally the physically stronger of the two. However, the two forwards do not have to operate like this in a 4-4-2, and you frequently see coaches deploy a withdrawn forward capable of playing in the 'hole' (the space on the field behind the main striker) and using their creative skills to set up opportunities for those around. When using the two forwards in this way it could be said that the formation is more of a 4-4-1-1 than a 4-4-2, and it is common to fluidly switch between these two formations depending on how the opposition is playing.

Strengths

+ Defensively, each player has another player nearby to help with their assignment, meaning that defenders have to cover less ground.

+ The short distance between the back line and the front line means there is less space for the opposition to work in.

+ The short distance between all three banks of players makes it easier to retain possession.

+ Playing with two forwards makes counter-attacking more effective.

+ Quick movement of the ball can often result in a two-on-two scenario in the opposition's penalty area.

+ Plenty of width for playing on the wing and making chances through crosses.

Weaknesses

- Using three flat lines makes it difficult to form triangle passing to cut the opposition open.

- Playing two central midfielders can lead to it becoming difficult to retain and gain possession in the midfield and can quickly lead to the midfielders becoming overwhelmed.

- If the lines don't stay compact and spread out too much, there will be lots of space for the opponent to operate in.

- If the fullbacks are pressing forward, it can create a lot of space for the opposition to counter attack.

4-2-3-1

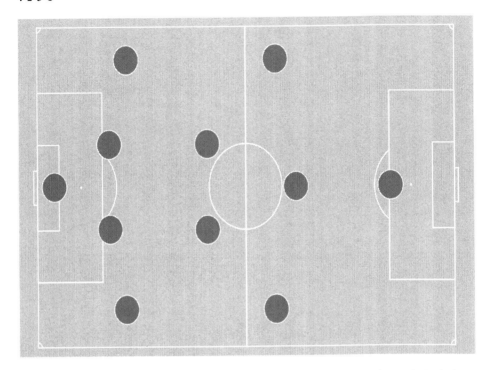

A slight variation on the 4-4-2 formation, the 4-2-3-1 formation came to prominence in Spain in the late 1990s and early 2000s and is now used by many teams around the world, replacing the 4-4-2 formation as the 'standard' formation in many of the top leagues.

This formation is all about getting numbers in and dominating the midfield, making it perfect to use if a team wants to slowly build an attack and dominate matches possession-wise.

- *Defensive Line*

The central defenders in a 4-2-3-1 generally play a similar role as in a 4-4-2 or a 4-5-1. Their main job is to repel attacks by tackling, heading, and marking opposition forwards either zonally or man-marking.

The fullbacks have the primary job of defending against the opposition's attackers, particularly wingers, and to stop the supply of balls into their own box for opposition forwards. It is beneficial that fullbacks have pace, as if they are up against a speedy winger they need to be able to keep up with them.

However, it is expected that the fullbacks will get forward to provide width when their team is attacking, and therefore they must also possess the ability to cross the ball and provide ammunition for the forwards.

- *Defensive Midfielders*

The defensive midfielders are vital to this formation as they provide the cover which allows the attacking players more freedom when in possession. One of the most important attributes a great defensive midfielder needs is positional sense so that they can protect the back four properly.

Generally, one of the two defensive midfielders will play the role of a ball winning midfielder and will have the job of winning the ball from the opposition to start an attack, while the other defensive midfielder will have the job of playmaker.

- *Attacking Midfielders*

The three attacking midfielders can make life very difficult for the opposition's defense, particularly if they interchange positions and make runs from deep. The three attacking midfielders generally line out with two wide players who are tasked with creating chances from the wing and one central playmaker who plays in behind the striker. But in a fluid version of this formation the wide players can drift inside, hug the touchline, and move wherever they please as well as constantly interchanging with the other two attacking midfielders.

It is also important for these three attacking midfielders to help out with defensive duties or their side will be outnumbered when the opposition attacks. Generally, when a side playing a 4-2-3-1 is defending they will revert to a 4-4-2 or a 4-4-1-1, with the two wide attacking midfielders moving deeper to help out the fullbacks.

- *Striker*

Although alone up front, the striker certainly doesn't lack support as there are three players behind whose job it is to create chances. If the three players are of genuine quality, this formation is a dream to the striker as they will see plenty of the ball and have plenty of chances throughout a game.

The formation can accommodate various types of strikers such as a tall and strong target player who can hold up the ball and feed the three attacking midfielders behind, or a small, more nimble striker who can make darting runs behind the defense and finish off the chances created. If the team is playing the formation with the intention of retaining possession and passing the ball to create chances, a target player who can hold up and lay off the ball is better suited, although if they are playing a counter attacking game, a quicker and more skillful striker might be better.

Strengths

+ Great formation for controlling the midfield with five players all operating in the middle of the park.

+ Reinforced defense when the opposition are in possession as they must get by two lines of defense (the defensive midfielders and central defenders) before getting through on goal.

+ Plenty of width from the fullbacks and wing players in the attacking midfield.

+ Can be used as a possession-based formation or as a counter attacking formation.

+ Allows for interchanging and roaming of forward players to confuse opposition's defense.

Weaknesses

- The forward player is left out on their own during midfield play and can be marked by both of the opposition's central defenders.

- Attacking midfielders must be willing to track back or else the defense will be outnumbered during an opposition attack.

- Attacking players can be quickly outnumbered if defensive midfielders constantly stay back.

- Can leave a lot of space between the defensive midfielders and attacking midfielder for the opposition to exploit.

4-5-1 (4-3-3)

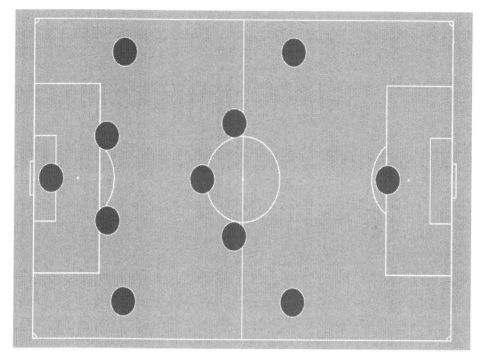

When using a 4-5-1 formation, the idea is to provide as much protection as possible to the defensive line and ensure there is as little space as possible in the defensive half for the opposition to work the ball.

When the opposition is in possession, the team playing 4-5-1 will generally have nine players behind the ball (ten including the goalkeeper) with the lone forward the only player on the halfway line or in the opposition's half. But when teams playing a 4-5-1 gain possession, they can quickly change to a 4-3-3 formation, providing plenty of attacking options and outnumbering the opposition's defense.

- *Defensive Line*

Regardless of which formation is used, the job of the central defenders remains largely unchanged, and they are always responsible for tackling, heading, and blocking in and around their own penalty area.

The fullbacks in a 4-5-1 or 4-3-3 formation must be able to both defend and attack. How much the fullbacks go forward is entirely dependent on the mentality of the team and if they are pushing forward for a goal or looking to defend a lead or a clean sheet. Fullbacks will need to help out the wide midfielders in a 4-5-1 formation, making overlapping runs and crossing the ball into the box for the lone forward and advancing midfielders. In a 4-3-3 formation, the onus on the fullback to get forward is even greater as they generally provide the majority of the play on the wings.

- *Defensive Midfielder*

In a 4-5-1 formation, the midfielder in the center of the five will generally be a defensive midfielder, playing just in front of the back four. This also applies to the center midfielder of the three in a 4-3-3 formation, with the defensive midfielder allowing the others to push forward when in possession.

This player must have similar attributes to a central defender as they must be able to tackle, break up the play, and have great positional awareness. When the defensive midfielder gains possession, they will generally look to one of the other midfielders to advance the play rather than moving forward with the ball themselves, instead playing a short pass and remaining in front of the back four.

- *All-Round Midfielders*

The two players flanking the defensive midfielder have the duty to both defend and attack, known as box-to-box midfielders. Their aim is to get into the opposition's penalty area when their team is in possession to provide options for a cross and to construct attacking moves by spreading the ball to the forwards, wingers or fullbacks. It is also possible to have one of the all-round midfielders playing as a playmaker, using their passing ability to split open the defense with a killer pass.

- *Wingers (Wide Attackers)*

Depending on whether a team is playing 4-5-1 or 4-3-3 they will have wingers or wide attackers. In a 4-5-1, the two outermost players in the midfield will operate as wingers and be under instruction to get forward regularly with speed when the team is in possession, as well as being asked to defend when the opposition is in possession.

But if a side is looking to attack and switch to a 4-3-3 formation, the wingers then become wide attackers and stay forward more often, using their pace and skill to beat defenders by cutting inside and running at the central defenders.

- *Striker*

In a 4-5-1, the striker is more isolated and therefore carries a greater burden to perform. It is crucial the lone striker possesses strength and skill with the ability to hold up the ball while the advancing midfielders and wingers come into play.

If the team is switching to a 4-3-3 and playing more attacking soccer, the burden on the striker is lessened, and the player can operate more as an out-and-out striker rather than a target player.

With two wide attackers either side, the main role of the striker in a 4-3-3 is to finish the chances that are created by their teammates.

Strengths

+ The formation is very fluid and can easily change from a defensive 4-5-1 to an attacking 4-3-3 throughout a game.

+ Solid defensive setup with a flat back four and a defensive midfielder.

+ Midfield is packed in a 4-5-1 creating less space for the opposition to work with and making it easier to close them down.

+ Plenty of width going forward in a 4-5-1 with fullbacks and wingers getting forward, similar in a 4-3-3 with fullbacks providing support for the wide attackers.

+ There are a number of players who can break from deep in a 4-5-1, quickly transitioning into a 4-3-3 and outnumbering the opposition's defense.

Weaknesses

- It is difficult to press the opposition in the final third using a 4-5-1 as players need to play deeper.

- If just using a 4-3-3, it is easy to become outnumbered in the middle of the park.

- Little protection afforded to the fullbacks when using a 4-3-3.

- Most attacks need to come from wide positions in a 4-5-1 due to lack of central support.

- The striker is isolated in a 4-5-1 so requires immediate support from advancing and box-to-box midfielders.

3-5-2

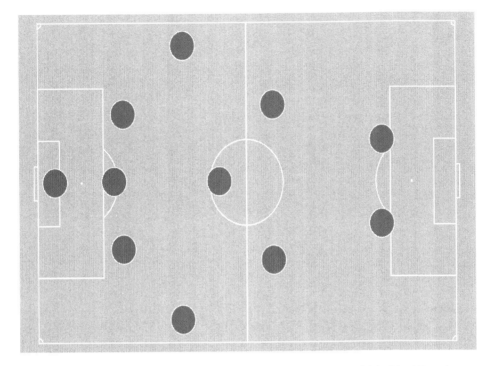

Many people say that matches are won or lost in the battle in midfield, and it is this philosophy that led to the creation of the 3-5-2 formation. The idea is to flood the midfield and use those extra bodies to create chances for the two forwards.

This is highly effective against a team playing 4-4-2 as it allows the team playing 3-5-2 to dictate the play and get more players forward. However, it can also be dangerous as the three central defenders can be left exposed out wide. It is therefore necessary to have three outstanding central defenders and two speedy wingbacks that can track back and help out when the opposition is attacking for this formation to be effective.

- *Defensive Line*

The defensive line consists of only three players, all of whom are generally central defenders. The central defenders must have great positional awareness as there are three players taking up the space where four players usually operate in a flat back four, so they must be aware of attacks coming in from the wing if the wingback can't get into position in time.

- *Wingbacks/Wingers*

Depending on how defensive or attacking a manager or coach wants to be, the two wide players will be asked to operate as wingbacks or wingers. If operating as wingbacks, the wide players will sit in between the central defenders and the central midfielders, moving back in line with the defense when the opposition has the ball and moving forward to provide width and crosses when their team is attacking.

If the team is playing a more attacking style, the wide players will operate more as wide midfielders or wingers, playing in line with the central midfielders and pushing forward more, leaving the main defensive responsibilities with the central defenders. When playing as a wide player in a 3-5-2 formation, it is vital to have great stamina and pace as there is a lot of running up and down the touchline involved.

- *Midfielders*

Generally, when implementing a 3-5-2 formation, there will be one defensive midfielder and two box-to-box midfielders, or one defensive midfielder, one attacking midfielder, and one ball-playing midfielder. Depending on how attack-minded the team is, two of the midfielders can push on behind the two forwards when in possession, offering plenty of options up front, and by making runs into the box can provide extra targets for the wingers to hit with their crosses.

The defensive midfielder can sit a little further up the field than one who is playing in front of a flat back four as there is already plenty of protection in the center of the field behind with three central defenders. It is common for the defensive midfielder to act as the ball playing midfielder in this formation, receiving the ball from one of the central defenders and picking out a more advanced player to start an attack.

- *Forwards*

It is common to play an advanced forward and a defensive or deep-lying forward in a 3-5-2 with one acting as a target player. Having an understanding between the two forwards is essential in this formation as if they both know instinctively where the other is going to be, they'll be able to create a lot of problems for the opposition defense.

The attributes for the forwards vary depending on the role being played, but the target player should generally be strong and able to deal with the opposition defense physically while the deep-lying forward should have explosive pace and acceleration to run onto through balls and past the opposition's defensive line.

Strengths

- + It is possible to create and develop a defending box between two of the central defenders and two of the midfielders to protect the central area where most goals are scored from.

+ Two forwards mean that the forward line isn't isolated and has a better chance of creating and scoring opportunities.

+ When breaking, a significant number of players can get forward quickly, outnumbering the opposition.

+ Allows for dominance of the midfield area with three midfielders in the middle and wingbacks operating out wide.

+ Great formation if wingbacks/wingers have strong crossing attributes as there should be at least two players in the box waiting for crosses.

Weaknesses

- Three central defenders make it tough to cover the width.

- Can be a very difficult formation to play.

- Wingbacks need to cover a huge amount of ground.

- Little protection on the wings with all other players operating centrally.

2.3 - Possession vs Long Ball

There are different ways of playing the beautiful game that we know and love, and it depends on your coach's own philosophy, and the players at their disposal, as to which brand of soccer your team is likely to play.

Possession

Possession-based soccer is simply about keeping the ball with short, sharp passes. The tempo is generally quite slow, and the ultimate aim is to tire out the opposition – who have to work harder to win back the ball – and slowly build attacks with players making incisive runs off the ball.

Possession soccer is based on the notion of 'pass and move', although in truth sometimes passing and then holding your position can be a great way to remain in space for the next phase of play. Keeping possession of the ball is one way of tiring out the opposition; so you don't want to be suffering from heavy legs yourself in the pursuit of the game.

Instead, play simple passes and keep your movements short and sharp. Everything needs to be done as quickly as possible – so try and bring the ball under control and pass it on with one or two touches, so that you can maximise the time that your teammates have in possession without being confronted by an opponent.

The beauty of playing this way is its simplicity. Make a simple pass and then move into space if you need to without 'leaving' your defensive position (e.g. if you are a central midfielder don't go bombing off over to the left wing if your position is not being covered by a teammate). Remember that retaining the ball is key, so whilst you would want to move forwards at all times, a pass sideways or backwards may be the better choice. Sometimes, a backward step can lead to two further forward.

Your first touch is crucial in the possession game, so work on this if necessary, as is an instinctive understanding of the situation around you. Where are your teammates and opponents? How much time do you have on the ball? Once you have a map in your mind, the game becomes so much easier to play.

There is a saying in soccer that 'if you haven't got the ball then you can't score'. With that in mind, perhaps possession-based soccer is the way forward!

The advantages of possession soccer:

+   Tires out the opposition, whilst keeping your team fresh.

+   Retaining possession stops opponents from dominating the game.

+   Slowly build attacks and creates space by pulling markers out of position.

+   Dictate the pace of the game.

+   Create chances through creative passing and movement off the ball.

The disadvantages of possession soccer:

-   Only certain players are effective in this system.

-   Can be hard to break down well-organized opponents.

-   A mistimed or misplaced pass can give possession back to the opposition in dangerous areas.

-   Not an effective system when your team needs quick goals, e.g. losing the match with 10 minutes to go.

Defending Against Possession

Defending against a team that is adept at keeping the ball can be tricky as their quick movements and rapid turnover of the ball are designed to pull you out of position. So remember the theory that the field can be broken down into specific zones, and that you have a zone to marshal relevant to your position.

If you play in central midfield then perhaps you say that the center circle is your zone or the third of the field in front of your defense. Then you need to command that area with sensible play – diving into sliding tackles when a team is able to knock the ball around at will around you is highly dangerous. So stay on your feet and make sure that you govern your zone effectively!

Long Ball

There is a common misconception that the long ball game is simply a tactic to get the ball up to a tall or strong striker as quickly as possible, and then build an attacking move around this player. Whilst this can be an effective tactic if you have such an individual in your team, the long ball can also be utilised to direct the ball into the 'channels', i.e. the areas of the field between fullbacks and center backs, for a fast striker or winger to sprint onto.

The long ball is a great way to a) take the pressure of your defenders, and b) create a counter-attacking opportunity. It can also be used wisely when the opposition packs their midfield with players, thus making them harder to break down.

The downside is that it can often leave the target player isolated, so make sure that they have adequate support around them when delivering the pass. A long ball to the head of a striker, who then heads it into the path of a fellow attacker, is one of the oldest tactics in the history of soccer, and whilst slightly outdated in these possession-based times, it can still be a hugely effective tactic.

The advantages of long ball soccer:

+ Benefit from a tall, strong or fast striker.

+ Takes pressure off the team's defenders.

+ Moves the team higher up the field.

+ Gets ball forward quicker – useful when needing a goal.

+ Can help to win free kicks and throw-ins in dangerous positions.

The disadvantages of long ball soccer:

- Passes need to be accurate, or the opposition will receive the ball.

- Can isolate attackers against opposition's defenders.

- Low ball retention means the team cannot dominate the game.

Defending Against a Long Ball

Defending against a long ball requires strength, toughness, awareness and an ability to react to 'second balls'. For long passes delivered to an attacker's head, you have to make a split-second decision:

Are you going to challenge for the ball and attempt to win it from them in the air?

or

Are you going to let them have the first ball and then either make sure that you nick it away from them before they can bring it under control?

or

Are you going to stay in position and cover any subsequent attacks?

You will need to judge the situation in order to make this decision, but use your own strengths as a guide: are you strong in the air, or is this attacker a particularly big player?

For a long ball delivered along the ground into a channel, you will need to be able to turn quickly and defend the space that the attacker will want to exploit. As explained in the Defending chapter, this is why giving yourself an extra yard or two when marking a pacey striker is crucial, as this will give you more time to get into a meaningful position to close them down.

Always be thinking about where the attacker wants the ball to be delivered, and what their next move is likely to be. This way you can plan ahead accordingly and take control of the situation.

2.4 - Pressing vs Defending Deep

How your team performs when they haven't got the ball is just as important as when they do have it. That might sound counter-intuitive, but think about it: if your defensive shape is all over the place then you will leave gaps for your opponents to exploit, and if you concede two or three goals per match then you leave yourselves a mountain to climb to get the win.

Defensive organisation and structure is hugely important, therefore. There are two broadly defined strategies that can be deployed, and which is best suited to your team depends on the nature of the players you have and how your team plays. But for you as an individual, it is imperative that you are aware of the distinct differences between the two. These are pressing and defending deep.

Pressing

This simply involves applying pressure to your opponents when they are in possession of the ball. Closing them down gives them less opportunity to play their natural game and get their passes away.

A pressing game is high energy, so it requires players with high levels of fitness and also needs individuals who understand the game well and are intuitive, rather than instinctive. There may be occasions when it isn't prudent to press your opponent as it could leave a teammate exposed, so understanding when and when not to press is also key.

It is also imperative that the team presses in formation together. So many goals are conceded when players don't press as a team and leave their defenders isolated. And that is the major disadvantage of the pressing game: it can leave space in dangerous areas which an intelligent attacker can exploit.

How to Play the Pressing Game

It goes without saying that the best way to defend is to make sure your opponents have the ball in their own half only: they can't score from there! By pressing them higher up the field, you are able to keep your defensive shape better whilst minimising the pressure on your own back line. A good pressing movement comes from all ten outfield players moving in time with one another – this is not about one teammate running around after the ball aimlessly.

The object of the pressing game is to win the ball back as quickly as possible. So whilst your team needs to close down the player in possession of the ball, you also need to close down their teammates and the space in which they have to work to effectively 'pen them in', and thus force them to give the ball away with a misplaced pass.

Good pressing is a two-fold idea: expect and react. So anticipate where the opponent is going to go with the pass – can you close down the space or intercept the pass? This is the reaction phase. Do not wait to see how the move unfolds; be proactive and press the ball as soon as you can. If all of your teammates are on the same page, then you will pressurise the opposition to give the ball away more times than not.

Advantages of pressing:

+   Gives the opposition less time on the ball.

+   Ability to win the ball back in dangerous areas.

+   Helps to facilitate an effective offside trap (when deployed correctly).

+   Pressing defenders can result in errors.

Disadvantages of pressing:

-    Can leave space in behind and in front of the defense.

-    Requires high energy and concentration.

-    Not always a good idea to press; needs players who can identify when and where.

Defending Deep

This is the ideal system for teams whose central defenders are tall and strong without much pace. By defending deep, you are eliminating the risk of an opponent's fast strikers using their pace to latch onto through balls. You may have heard the term 'park the bus' used before, and that essentially refers to teams that defend deep and get all 11 players behind the ball.

At the other end of the field, in a deep defending set-up your attackers will drop further back into midfield and allow the opposition's defenders to have possession of the ball. The idea behind this is that they are less effective than their midfielders, so cutting off the supply line makes perfect sense. It is so much harder to launch an attack when the defending team has organized themselves into an almost impenetrable wall.

Though, defending deep can give the opposition more time on the ball in the final third. This can be dangerous as it allows creative talents more time to pick out a pass or shot. That said, by utilising tight defensive lines it is possible to minimise the amount of space available.

Advantages of Defending Deep:

+   Minimises threat of speedy strikers.

+   Cuts off ball supply from defense to midfield.

+   Helps to restrict the creation of chances.

Disadvantages of Defending Deep:

-    Gives opponents more time on the ball.

- Can be hard to mount attacks of your own from a deep position.

- Invites continuous pressure.

It is likely that the characteristics of you and your teammates will dictate which defensive strategy your coach employs. If they prefer to press, then you will need to ensure you have good stamina levels and that your timing in interceptions and tackling are good. Your positional sense and awareness of those around you will also be tested. For a good insight into pressing done well, watch Barcelona or Bayern Munich in action.

If your coach prefers defending deep, then you will need to know exactly who you are supposed to be marking or the zones which are yours to command. Listening to the communications of those around you will also help.

2.5 - Counter Attack

Picture the scene: you've been defending for your lives for the past 89 minutes. Your opponents have committed plenty of bodies forward, but suddenly give the ball away in your half of the field. This could be your one and only chance to win this game. Now is the time to hit them on the counter-attack....

A counter attack is literally that: hitting your opponents on the break when they have committed to attacking your goal. It usually involves either a direct ball or a series of swift passes that maneuver the ball from in your half to a dangerous position in your opponents' in the shortest possible timeframe, catching them unawares.

When to Counter Attack

Timing a counter attack correctly is crucial. It can be a fantastic way to sneak a late goal when your opponents are pushing to score themselves, but push too many players forward in your counter-strike and you may find yourselves vulnerable to a counter-attack.

The best time to counter attack is when defending set pieces. This is because your opponents are likely to send a number of players into your penalty area, with two or three left back on the halfway line as defensive insurance. So it's worth leaving one or two of your fastest players forward to exploit the extra space this creates.

A counter-attacking strategy is a good one where you are up against a really strong opposition. It may be the best chance you have of getting anything from the game – keeping a good defensive shape and only throwing a few players forward at opportune moments. There have been plenty of examples of 'smash and grab' raids like these over the years!

On a similar note, it is a good idea to play on the counter-attack when you have been reduced to ten players due to a red card or injuries.

Counter Attack Strategies

• Quick Break

The key to an effective counter attack is quite often pace. It is the one attribute that terrifies defenders, and also enables you to get the ball further up the field in the least possible time, which minimises the chances of defenders getting back to fend off your attack.

The key to the Quick Break strategy is withdrawing into your own half of the field and thus inviting your opponents forward. The secret is to leave some of your quick players in advanced positions, either centrally or out wide. Then, when you manage to win the ball back, knock a ball forward for your pacey attackers to run on to. This should signal a charge forward from two or three teammates; with the ultimate aim of creating a goalscoring opportunity before the opposition have had a chance to funnel back.

The Quick Break tactic is perfect for those who are playing defensively against a strong team or to protect a lead, or where your formation leaves one player high up the field and playing on the shoulder of the last defender.

• The Midfield Steal

The Midfield Steal is a two-part process: step one, a midfielder will steal the ball from an opponent in much the same vein as in the Quick Break, e.g. defending deep and in numbers.

Step two is then that the midfielder will look around and deliver a long pass to an advancing teammate. A good striker or winger will anticipate that once the midfielder has stolen possession, they need to make an intelligent run at speed into space. This should create a one-on-one or two-on-one situation if timed correctly.

• Set Piece Siege

The premise behind the Set Piece Siege is that you are gambling on your goalkeeper claiming the ball. One he or she has, the onus is then on two or three of the quickest players on your team charging forward into space to receive the ball.

2.6 - The Offside Trap

The offside trap has proven to be a godsend for defenders who have had a nightmare stopping pacey strikers from latching onto through balls. Imagine defending against a striker with the pace of a 100m sprinter when a player is about to slide a defense-splitting pass to them! It would be impossible to stop them ordinarily, but that all changed when some clever soul invented the offside trap.

It revolves around a defensive unit of three, four or five (the fewer players there are, the lower the risk) moving up in tandem in a straight line when the call is made. This then, hopefully, leaves the attackers in an offside position when the ball is played through.

When deployed correctly, all of the defenders move up in unison at the same time. When deployed badly, one defender is left behind and plays all of the attackers onside – usually with devastating consequences.

It might sound tricky, but with plenty of work on the training ground a thriving offside trap can be achieved. With focus, concentration and understanding, you can play your part in keeping the opposition at bay with ease.

Keys to a Successful Offside Trap

Really, an offside trap will live or die through the communication between defenders. Get this bit right and deploying the offside trap will become instinctive, almost second nature. But with poor communication and timing, the whole thing can fall down like a pack of cards, and leave the attacking side with the easiest of chances.

So nominating a center back with intelligence and intuition to be the decision-maker is vital. And make sure they are loud too! If nobody can hear their call to step up then the whole system will be flawed from the outset.

Anticipating the right moment to deploy the offside trap is, as it goes without saying, crucial. If your opposition play a lot of long balls, then it can be easier to spot when the time is right to move out as a unit. If, on the other hand, if they are more of a shorter, quick tempo passing side, then choosing the right moment can be much harder to predict.

So against certain opposition, the offside trap can be played with more confidence than against others. Picking a leader who recognises this fact, and then discussing whether the tactic should be used together as a defensive unit, is of paramount importance.

The Do's and Don'ts of the Offside Trap

Here is a quick checklist of the things to practise and avoid when undertaking an offside trap:

+ Do appoint a loud, communicative, intelligent center back as offside trap 'leader.'

+ Do confirm that the whole defensive unit is aware of their role and requirements prior to deploying the trap.

+ Do practise it religiously on the training field before using it in a match.

- Don't appoint a leader who struggles with concentration.

- Don't appoint a leader who is shy – they need to be prepared to shout the houses down!

- Don't deploy the trap unless you are 100% certain everyone is up to speed.

- Don't deploy the trap when you are winning with five minutes to go – why take the risk?

2.7 - Communication

It shouldn't be underestimated how important communication is out on the field. Whether it is verbal messaging or visual, the way teammates interact with one another on the field can go a long way to separating success and failure.

Soccer is unpredictable, and so support and guidance is often needed as the game ebbs and flows. Sometimes, just simple encouragement will suffice.

And of course, there are the technical sides to effective communication too – letting your teammate know they have a 'man on' (a player approaching them from behind to take the ball off them), or that you're in acres of space, are both examples of how being on the same wavelength as your colleagues can pay huge dividends.

The reality is that however good a player is, they only have a limited amount of time on the ball and peripheral vision to see what is going on around them. This is where extra communication is vital. Who knows….it might just get you a goal some day.

Some Common (English) Soccer Phrases

Each language has its own vernacular of course, but for English speakers, there are numerous stock phrases and words you can use to help communicate with your teammates.

'Man On / Behind you' – this is a classic phrase that lets your teammate know that an opponent is closing in on them to make a tackle. None of us have eyes in the back of our head, and often in cramped midfield battles the 'man on' shout is much needed.

'Back Post/Front Post' – this one can work at both ends of the field. Defensively, it lets your fellow defenders know where to go when players need marking just prior to a set piece being delivered into the penalty area. From an attacking perspective, it can also lead a wide player to know where you want the ball to be delivered when you're charging into the box.

'Show him/her inside/outside' – you may have noticed the way in which an attacker likes to play. Maybe they are extremely strong on their right foot but weak on their left? In this instance, you would shout to a teammate to show him or her onto that weaker side.

'Drop back' – this can be a particularly useful shout from defenders to midfielders when they feel they aren't getting adequate support. It can also be used when a tactical change from a pressing system to deep defending is necessary.

'Time' – let your teammates know when they are in space and no challenger is nearby. This will help them to relax in possession and pick the right pass.

'Squeeze' or 'Press' - if this command is directed towards you then you will be expected to close down the opponent with the ball in order to minimise their space.

'Get in there / Challenge' – as it sounds, this implies that you need to put a tackle in on your opponent. A teammate will ask you to 'get in there' or 'challenge' when they feel there is adequate defensive cover for you so that you are free to attack the ball without fear of being dragged out of position.

'Away / Clear' – when a ball is delivered into your penalty area a command of 'away' or 'clear it' may come from a fellow defender or your goalkeeper. This simply means that you need to get rid of the ball as far away from your goal as possible using either foot or your head.

'Contain' – the contain call will let you and your teammates know that you are in a potentially dangerous scenario out on the field, e.g. maybe your defense is temporarily outnumbered by the opposition's attack. To contain your opponent's adequately, you must hold your position and jockey any player that enters your defensive zone until reinforcements work their way back to support you.

'Cover me / Covered' – the 'cover me' shout denotes that a teammate is about to leave their normal position and that they want you to fill in the space they leave. This can happen when a defender steps out to challenge an opponent, or when a central midfielder asks a striker to cover them when they move out wide to close down an opponent. The call of 'covered' lets you know that if you find yourself in any of the scenarios outlined, you will be supported by a teammate who will temporarily occupy your position for you.

Visual Communications

There are times when verbal communication isn't required, and a simple hand gesture or change in body language will suffice.

Pointing into space – this lets your teammate know where you want the ball to be delivered. This is particularly useful for a striker running the channels or a winger making a run inside their marker.

Pointing to the head – this is similar to the above, in that it lets your teammates know where you want the ball to be delivered. Commonly used at free kicks and corners.

Holding up a number of fingers – this is a signal used by goalkeepers to show how many players they want to form a defensive wall when the opponents have been awarded a free kick in a dangerous area.

Praying – this is the signal used when you have mistimed a tackle and you don't want to be booked by the referee!

Leading from the Front

Being appointed captain of your team is a huge honor, and with it comes great responsibility. You will need to lead from the front, as you will be the heartbeat of your team.

Most captains are appointed because of their vocal nature and will to win. They motivate the team to do well, provide guidance and encouragement when things aren't going well and lead from the front when things are. They will also, crucially, promote an environment of positivity and security, and make sure that none of their teammates are blighted by the dreaded 'fear of failure'.

You will also be the coach's on-field mouthpiece, relaying new tactics and ideas in the middle of the game; so tactical awareness is a must too. You are, in effect, his or her lieutenant, and you should take the time to talk to them one-to-one to check you fully understand the tactics they want to employ.

2.8 - Research Your Opponent

Preparation is the key to soccer success, and being able to out-think your opponents will lead you on the path to glory.

It's always good to do your homework on each and every team you play. If you can get the opportunity to watch them play in the flesh then great; take a notebook and write down anything that stands out to you – strengths, weaknesses. Areas your team will need to improve on or exploit. For example, if your opponents are a small team, make sure you practise plenty of set-piece deliveries – it could be the difference between winning and losing.

If you can't get to watch them live then make sure you study the league table and their most recent results. Do they concede a lot of goals or not many at all? Do they score plenty or few? Do they perform well at home or away....or both? Do they concede/score early or late goals often? All of these little insights will help you to prepare thoroughly for how your opponents will play and the tactics they will deploy.

If anything of note comes out of your research, then make sure you inform your coach and hopefully you will then get the opportunity to prepare thoroughly in advance of the match in training.

'By failing to prepare, you are preparing to fail'. The former American president Benjamin Franklin said that, and he couldn't be more right. Do your homework on your opponents and you will have the opportunity to comprehensively out-think them before a ball has even been kicked.... and half the battle will already be won.

Chapter 3

Attackers

The glamour position in soccer, attackers are the players expected to assist and score the majority of goals for their team. Doing this requires a brave, tough, and aggressive mentality as defenders are built and designed to stop attackers at any cost. It also requires 100% focus, with attackers having to be ready to pounce on the smallest mistake from an opposition defender.

Every time the ball enters the offensive zone, an attacker should have the main priority and mindset to create an opportunity and get a shot on target. Ideally, every time an attacker receives the ball they will have enough time and space to place a shot on goal. But this doesn't always happen, so it's also important to aggressively maintain possession, fight for optimal field position, and bring their teammates into play.

The true beauty of being an attacker lies in the ability to be so many different things, all of which are inherently different but have the same endgame – to create or score a goal. You can head the ball into the goal, strike from outside the box, or time your runs, all with the same effect.

If you've decided that becoming an attacker is your goal, you need to decide which traits are you're strongest and which traits you need to work on. Some of the most useful traits include:

- Inch-Perfect Decision Maker

It is possible for attackers to spend a large chunk of the game without the ball at their feet, but it is important to remain entirely focused and ready the second an opportunity arises. Should you shoot? Should you try to dribble past a defender? Or maybe you should try a killer pass? These are all the questions that an inch-perfect decision maker has to answer in a split second. The answers to these questions can often decide entire matches.

- Powerful Player

When talking about a powerful attacking player, it is a reference to their ability to threaten from outside the 18 yard box. If an attacking player is a threat outside the box as well as inside the box, they will be far more dangerous around the goal and will make the defenders respect the fact they can score from anywhere on the field. Having this trait will usually make the opposition's defenders come out a bit more and leave space in behind them or make the opposition play a defensive midfielder and sacrifice an attacking player.

- Speedy Player

A team that possesses speedy forwards who can run at defenders, beat them in a foot race and get onto crosses and through balls first can be lethal. No matter where the ball is, a speedster has the capability to get there first and create a chance. This trait is especially common in wingers and wide midfielders who can run with pace down the wing or cut inside and use their pace to terrify defenses.

- Masterful Ball Control

A player who possesses masterful ball control can hold up play and keep defenders at bay. Instead of running all over the field to create space and chances, they have the technical ability to bring down difficult balls and 50/50 balls with ease, becoming a target for their team when they are trying to get rid of the ball from the defensive area. A forward with this trait can hold up the ball while the rest of the team catches up.

- Lethal Finisher

Having a lethal finish is a hugely important trait, and while the player may not be the strongest or quickest player on the field, they will constantly dazzle and amaze with their intelligence and timing. They have the ability to show up in the right place at the exact right time and clinically finish the ball out of the goalkeeper's reach.

- Instinctual

The instinctual player can create something out of nothing, produce minor miracles on a regular basis, and makes up many of the highlights in the highlight reel. When this player is in possession of the ball in the final third, the crowd holds their breath in anticipation as they squeeze through the smallest of spaces, out-dribble defenders, and create chances out of nothing. These players don't feel pressure, even on the biggest occasions, and remain cool, calm, and collected every time they receive the ball.

- Incredible Aerial Ability

Players who possess incredible aerial ability live to be airborne and base their game around their foreheads. Often, these players are quite tall, are able to reach into the free space above the ground and demand to be the focus of attention from set pieces and corners. Additionally, they provide crucial height and aerial skills when their side is defending a set piece or corner.

3.1 - Attacking Midfielders and Wingers

Attacking midfielders and wingers (or side midfielders) are by nature extremely talented with the ability to create several clear-cut chances during a match. They are expected to be an offensive threat every time they touch the ball, either by creating goalscoring opportunities for others or by attempting a shot themselves.

These players are the link between the center midfield line and the forward line, operating in between the opposition's defensive and midfield lines, and are often the most exciting players on the field to watch.

Playing as an Attacking Midfielder or Winger

- Feed the Strikers

Your main objective as an attacking midfielder or winger is to create chances for your teammates, primarily your strikers. Different strikers have different strengths, so you must take the time to understand how they like the ball to be delivered in order to maximise the goalscoring potential of your team. If your striker is tall and/or good in the air, then floated deliveries that they can attack are the best option. For smaller strikers and those who are good finishers, whipped crosses or through balls in behind will give them the best possible opportunity to get a shot away without being beaten in the air by a taller defender.

If you are operating in mainly central areas, then the same principles still apply. Strong attackers who are perhaps lacking in pace won't want to be trying to chase down through balls, whereas small strikers won't want to be the physical focal point of attacks. Knowing the attackers' strengths will help to optimise your game too, and minimise the number of wasted balls played.

So if your striker loves getting on the end of crosses, stay as wide as you can to maximise your space and increase the chances of you finding yourself isolated in a one-on-one situation against a defender. If your team doesn't carry much of a physical threat, then don't be afraid to drift inside to try and slide a few through balls beyond the defense.

- Risk and Reward

Making the right decisions in the right areas at the right time can unlock a defense and create an opening – crucial in a tight match where few chances have been created. Knowing when to run at a defender and take them on with your dribbling skills or pace is as important as knowing when not to take the risk, and thus opting instead to retain possession. As a player charged with creating goalscoring opportunities, you won't get it right every time, and may find yourself losing possession on occasion. But it only takes one bit of skill or one crafty pass to create a goal, so remain confident and keep trying the unexpected.

The ultimate reward for your risk is a goal for you or a teammate, so don't be disheartened if things don't initially go your way. At the same time, you have to know when the right time is to take a risk. If your team is 1-0 up with 15 minutes to play, then is the risk worth the reward? What happens if you give the ball away and the opposition go down the other end and snatch an equalising goal? Sometimes, it is better to play within yourself and maintain what you have. But, generally speaking, you are there to make things happen as an attacking player, so take the risk and enjoy the reward when it comes.

- Be Positive, Play Forward

In the modern game, many coaches adopt a 'keep the ball at all costs' mentality, which means passing the ball backwards or sideways in order to recycle possession. But as you know, you need to be within 30 meters of your opponents' goal to score! (generally speaking). So maintaining positivity in possession is a crucial feature of any effective attacking players' game. Of course, there will be times when you have to knock the ball back to your supporting fullback or inside to a midfielder, but always ensure that your next movement is a forward one into space in order to help your team progress up the field.

When you receive the ball, get your head up and always look forwards. Hopefully, your attacking teammates are offering you an option, but if not see if you can manufacture a situation where you isolate yourself against a single defender. In this scenario, you can use your skill, power or pace to find a way past them. By being positive and playing forward more often than not, you will provide an effective outlet for your team, alleviate the pressure on your defenders and create more openings rather than the 'pass it back or sideways' merchants who look effective but actually don't offer any real cutting edge to their team.

- Aim for the Gaps

The one ball that defenders hate to deal with more than any other is the one slid into a gap. This means that they have to turn and run, whilst the attacker, who should already be on their toes and facing towards the opponent's goal, will have an instant advantage. This is the same for wingers and attacking midfielders when they are hunting for space, aim for the gaps by running into the channels between defenders and midfielders.

As a winger, you may find that the space is on the outside of them: sprint into it and prompt your midfielder to pass the ball. As an attacking midfielder, you may often struggle to find space due to the amount of 'traffic' in the middle of the field. So, once again, aim for the gaps: pull left or right, drop a bit deeper or push higher up. The ideal positioning is in the line between the defense and midfield, as neither of these two units will know which is supposed to be marking you.

- Stay on the Move

The easiest opponent to mark is one who remains stationary at all times, and who is therefore predictable in their work. So it's important that you stay on the move in order to eliminate the risk of being picked up with ease by your marker. Wingers can come short before spinning and running in behind their fullback. They can cut inside and make a run into the channel between the fullback and the central defender – these are just two ideas to add an air of unpredictability to your game.

As an attacking midfielder you will have to work harder to find space, and so staying on the move is critical. Remember to operate within 'the lines', e.g. between the defenders and the midfield, to buy yourself more time in possession. If you watch a game of professional soccer, make a note of how many times an attacking midfielder receives the ball in a pocket of space before slipping a pass to a teammate or firing a shot at goal. This is one of the most effective creative outlets for your team, so remember that movement is the key.

- Track Back!

In the vast majority of cases, wingers and attacking midfielders will be tasked with defensive duties too, and the key instruction will be to track back to support your defensive players. A winger will need to work closely with their fullback to negate the effect of their opponent's wide players, as 'doubling up' will help to minimise the risk of the opponent's having an advantage in wide areas.

And with more and more teams flooding the midfield with bodies, an attacking midfielder will need to drop deep to support the midfield unit in winning the battle in the middle of the field. An attacking player who neglects their defensive role is thought of as being lazy and not working for the team.

3.2 - Strikers

A striker is the focus of any team's attack, stationed in the offensive half of the field and possessing technical skills, good movement, tactical awareness, and of course shooting ability.

It is common for strikers to find themselves outnumbered and surrounded by the opposition's defense, and therefore never giving up on the ball is an important trait. They must keep working to cause problems for the opposition when they have the ball, and create space and find openings in the defensive line when they don't. Assertiveness and confidence are both essential, especially when asked to play a lone role up front.

Playing as a Striker

- Know your Suppliers

As a striker, getting to know your teammates strengths is a brilliant way to give yourself an advantage in the final third of the field. Do your wingers like to get their head up and cross early, or are they the sort that likes to beat their marker and get to the by-line? Do they float their crosses or whip them in? Knowing this information will enable you to gain an advantage over your marker, by allowing you to time your run and instinctively know where the ball will be travelling to. And what about your midfield players: do they like to hit early balls into the channels, or do they prefer a slow build up before they find that killer pass? Again, this will enable you to keep your wits about you and plan your movements effectively.

It makes sense then to tailor your runs to the strengths of the player in possession. If you possess a playmaker in your team that is capable of spraying long balls accurately, then let them know you are available to receive the ball – either by pointing into the space you want to exploit or by gaining a yard on your opponent and calling for the ball. If you aren't lucky enough to have such a creative talent around you; not to worry, you will need to be patient and wait for the opportunities to come along. But the bottom line is that knowing your teammates' games inside out will benefit your own performances.

- Be the First to Everything

In soccer, the first five yards of any movement are the most critical. If you can get a yard or two of space then you can make things happen: whether that's receiving the ball and linking the play, or having more time to get your shot away in a crowded penalty area. By establishing the ability to move sharply in short bursts, you should be the first to every ball; including dangerous crosses and clever passes.

In time, this will become instinctive, almost telepathic: you will know what's about to happen and your body will kick into gear. This could be the difference between meeting that cross cleanly or being muscled off the ball by a defender. So work on your sharp bursts of speed – resistance training and shuttle sprints are great practice for this – and let your instinct for goals take over on the field.

- Timing is Key

Great timing can be the difference between a goal and a defender clearing the ball, the difference between a well-timed tackle and a free kick being given away. For strikers, timing is so important. You can gain an extra yard or two on a defender by timing a run effectively, and when you are trying to create opportunities for yourself that can be crucial. Good timing enables smaller attackers to beat tall defenders in the air too: when the ball is in wide areas you want to position yourself behind a defender so they can't see you – it's human nature for them to become uncertain then. As your winger is about to deliver the ball then you make your move; darting in front of the defender to give yourself a clear leap at the cross.

The same principle applies to passes made through the middle of the field too. Give yourself a yard of space by peeling away from your marker with your body in a side on position to the player in possession, and then holler for the ball – pointing into the space you want to receive it is a good trick. If timed well, this will again give you a huge advantage. Remember, the ball is in your court, you are the one that holds all the aces as the defender has to mark you, not the other way around. So work on your timing to gain the ultimate advantage.

- Surprise Surprise

Be unpredictable – that is great advice for any aspiring striker. The minute you become predictable is the moment that your marker will have a field day; knowing exactly what you are about to do next before you have even done it. By offering up a few surprises, both in your movement and with the ball at your feet, ensures that the opposition will have a torrid time trying to mark you out of the game.

So think about your movement: standing still, or repeating the same move time and time again, is predictable. By changing your trigger movements – dropping deep, running into the space in behind, pulling left or right – you can make your marker's life a misery. They will become tired physically and mentally with trying to keep up, and like the predator you are then you can strike.

And being able to surprise and outfox your marker with the ball at your feet is key too. Being unpredictable – but not just for the sake of it; actually producing a positive pass or shot – is highly advantageous. With this in mind, make sure you regularly practise with your weaker foot. If you pick the ball up and want to get a shot away, but favour your right foot heavily, then your opponent will know how to close you down. But if you possess the ability to strike the ball as well with either foot, then you can drop your shoulder in either direction to create a yard of space – and defenders hate having to deal with this!

- Sniff out Weaknesses

Every defender has their own weaknesses, and the sooner you can sniff these out in a match then the sooner you will be able to cash in on them. But the onus is on you to test them out, so make sure you try different things early in the match where possible. Ask for the ball to be played in behind; did your marker show a good turn of pace? Get balls played into you aerially – did your marker look good in the air or possess a good jump? And watch him or her in possession too; are they comfortable on the ball, or if you closed them down quickly enough would they make a mistake? All of these considerations need to be noted, as one moment of weakness on a defender's part could leave you with an opportunity to score.

Of course, the weakness may be a collective one, rather than individually. Make a mental note as to how well your opponent's defensive unit works; is their offside trap well drilled? If not, you may find yourself through on goal and in acres of space with a well-timed run. Do they defend deep or high up the field? If they defend high then again you can get in behind courtesy of a well-placed pass. If they defend with a deep line then that could open up space in front of them – allowing you the chance to drop a bit deeper and pick up possession. Remember, identifying weaknesses can turn a defeat into a draw, and a draw into a victory in one quick moment of inspiration.

- Stay Calm

Staying cool, calm and clinical is another attribute that is much sought-after in a good striker. Often you will have the blink of an eye to shoot or make a pass before a defender closes you down, and so remaining calm in the face of a fast-paced landscape is important. The very best strikers in the world are the ones who finish coolly even when they have a horde of defenders closing in on them.

Of course, you can improve your own sense of calm by being well prepared before you take to the field. Knowing instinctively what you will do in any given situation can help to turn you into an ice cold goalscoring machine, so repetition in training helps a lot.

Remember, when you receive the ball, you are in control of the situation. The defenders will be nervous of making a tackle because if they get it wrong then your team could win a penalty or a free kick in a dangerous area. Once you get into the mindset that you are in control, you will feel a lot calmer than your marker!

The same is true when you find yourself clean through on goal in a one-on-one situation with the goalkeeper. You are the active party, whilst the keeper is the reactive one. They don't know what you are going to do – whether that's shoot early, try to chip them or dribble the ball around them – and so they are simply reacting to your move. As a striker, this gives you enormous power and ensures you are the master of your own destiny.

Chapter 4

Midfielders

Known as the 'engine of the team', midfielders are generally positioned on the field in between the defensive line and the forwards and are tasked with the job of controlling the play both defensively and offensively. In modern soccer, some midfielders play a more defensive role while others blur the boundaries between midfield and forward, however, all midfielders must possess both defensive and attacking qualities as they will be expected to fulfill both roles at certain stages throughout a match.

What role a midfielder takes on is determined by the formation and tactic implemented by the manager or coach, with the number of midfielders on a team varying between, although not limited to, two and five. Formations can be written to signal a single midfield line such as 4-4-2, 4-3-3, or 3-5-2 or can be written to signal two midfield lines such as 4-2-3-1 or 4-1-3-2.

The key to this position is versatility as midfield players have to have the defensive qualities to help out their back line and the attacking qualities to create and finish goal opportunities. Some midfielders are requested to think defensively first and these are known as defensive midfielders, while others are tasked with both attacking and defending duties and are known as center midfielders.

Regardless of which role a manager or coach requests, all midfielders must have the following qualities:

- High Levels of Fitness

The demands of the midfield position require covering the full length of the field – going back to help out the defensive line when the opposition are in possession, or moving forward to create or finish an opportunity when your team is in possession. There are few other players on the field who run as much as midfielders and as such they must be among the fittest on their team and perhaps some of the fittest athletes in any team sport.

- Vision and Creativity

Midfielders must be able to pick the correct pass when in possession and have the intelligence and creativity to thread through passes to more advanced players. Your team could be full of top attackers constantly finding gaps in the oppositions' midfield and defense, but if the midfielders lack the vision and creativity to survey the movements and spaces, and lay on the pass, then all the attacks will come to nothing. Having the ability to make clever passes that no-one else sees can be the difference maker in a close match.

- Understand the Role of Teammates

This is an important quality for all players in a soccer team. But it is especially true for midfielders who must understand when the fullbacks, wingers, or forwards are going to make a run into a threatening position. Similarly, it is important to understand when a central defender is going to make a foray forward and requires cover. Midfielders must understand how their teammates play and what their roles are in order to fulfill their roles properly.

- Enjoy Having the Ball At Your Feet

Unlike central defenders who generally have average ball skills and seek to get rid of the ball as soon as they receive it, midfielders should feel comfortable in possession, be able to take some time on the ball to seek a good pass, and should have great technical skills such as dribbling and ball handling, but especially passing. Midfielders are the 'possession players' of their side and as such should always be comfortable with the ball at their feet, even when under pressure.

4.1 - Center Midfielders

To put it simply, the center midfielder is the 'brain' of any soccer team, and the hub of the team, keeping the side ticking over both in and without possession.

In possession, a center midfielder must maintain the rhythm of the game, keeping the passing crisp and quick or slowing the game down to a more suitable tempo. They must be able to link every single player on the field, passing, directing the play, and leading by example.

There is no one type of mold that is perfect for a center midfielder as the player must be able to perform multiple tasks. Whether small, quick, tall, or lanky, great center midfielders come in all shapes and sizes. Some of the best in the world are of differing physiques, yet all bring so much to their teams through their understanding of the game and ability to perform in the middle of the park at the absolute highest level.

Playing as a Center Midfielder

- Positioning

As you are the heartbeat of your team in the middle of the park, it is vital that you are in the right place at all times. If you are caught out of position, your opponents are likely to have a wealth of space to exploit, and this could leave your midfield partner(s) in a two-on-one or three-on-two situation.

As is indicative of the central midfield role, you have to work your way into good positions both defensively and in attack. So make sure you are adding value to your defensive unit; whether you act as a shield in front of your defenders, or if you are tasked to close down the opposition's midfielders and stop them from dictating play, it is imperative that you occupy the right position to achieve this goal.

From an offensive perspective, whilst you should adopt a central position there is no harm in moving slightly wider in order to support your teammates in creating goalscoring opportunities. If you see space that could lead to something, run into it. Despite your billing as a central midfielder, you are not shackled to the center circle – most of the best midfielders in the world will move around with freedom.

This is particularly the case in the modern game, where many coaches look to 'flood' the middle of the field with players, which minimises the amount of space on offer to creative talents. So instead look to play 'in the layers' – you could drop deep to receive possession and create space that way, or try to float into areas beyond the opposition midfield. For a strong central midfield, positional sense is crucial.

- Don't be Predictable

Many matches are decided by a single moment of brilliance. Whether it's a killer pass, a long range shot or an off the ball run that creates space for a teammate, being unpredictable is, predictably, a great skill to have at your disposal. Playing the same passes, and making the same old runs, is a sure fire way for your opponents to be able to predict what you are about to do next. This in turn will enable them to shut you down with ease. So sometimes it is beneficial to think outside the box or carry out a move that they will not be expecting.

Alternate your passing; try along the floor and over the top, and try different runs too, like bursting from deep and arcing into wider positions. It is also well worth popping up in different pockets of space, whether that means occupying a deeper position or supporting your attackers more closely.

- Conserving Energy

Central midfield is the most physically demanding position on the field, as you will be expected to cover a lot of ground both defensively and in supporting attacking moves. So knowing when to make that lung-bursting run, and knowing when to conserve your energy is vital. This is aided if you play in midfield with a partner with whom you can alternate roles, so for example, they will be the energetic one for a while as you take a breather.

Even when you are tired, at the very least make sure that you perform your defensive duties and keep your shape. Many canny central midfielders will hold their position in the middle of the park when tired, to avert the risk of making a run forward and not having the legs to get back and support your defense should your team lose possession.

A good way to conserve energy without impacting upon your performance is to try to read the game intently. This will allow you to predict where the ball is going to go, the runs your teammates will make and the space your opponent will burst into. By seeing the game early, you can get into position without needing to sprint at full pace to get there. Preparation is often the best way to conserve energy, whilst still engaging with the game in defense and attack.

- Stay a Step Ahead

The very best central midfielders are the ones who can see the game unfolding in front of them, and as such are able to stay one step ahead of proceedings. It's like the old chess grandmasters who are working three moves ahead at all times. As soon as you receive the ball in midfield, you should know where your teammates are, which runs they are likely to make and where your opponents are. Build a map of the field in your mind as the game unfolds, and don't be afraid to look up and around just before you receive the ball, as this will buy you time.

Getting used to playing in tight spaces, where time on the ball is at a premium will help you, so try the old 'piggy in the middle' style games on the training ground. Of course, possessing a good first touch will enable you to have an extra second or two on the ball – great for picking out that killer pass. And decision-making is also a skill that will allow you to stay one step ahead of the opposition - a brilliant attribute for a central midfielder to have.

- Long Range Shooting

As you dictate the play from the middle of the field you may find opportunities to shoot when you are 20/25 yards from goal in central areas. This could be from a static position – you are in control of the ball but cannot see a good pass or your teammates aren't making effective runs into space – or from an active position, where perhaps a ball has deflected to you during an attack or you have burst on to a pass.

Often, you will only have a split second to react in a game, so whilst it pays to practise your long range shooting in training, you will often need to rely on gut instinct during a match. So take in some of your surroundings before the first whistle is blown: is the opposition's goalkeeper exceptionally small or tall in size? A small goalkeeper will struggle with shots hit into the top corners, whilst a tall goalkeeper may struggle to get down in time to low shots. And use the field to your advantage: if the grass is slightly wet, the ball will actually accelerate off the surface, adding another problem for the keeper to contend with. On rainy days often low shots are a great idea.

- Timing your Runs

In life, timing is everything – and that is certainly the case when playing as a central midfielder too. When the ball is fed wide to your wingers, you have a decision to make: when do I make my run into the penalty area? If you run too early, you will be easier to mark and may not find yourself in the optimum position for the delivery into the box. Make your run too late, and you may miss out on the action altogether. So timing is key, as is the position you take up.

Keep a close eye on your winger, and try to start your move just as he or she is about to release the ball. As you make your move, have a picture in your mind of where you want to be. Do you want to be the primary attacker of the ball, or do you want to be engaged in the second phase of play? You have to ask yourself these questions all over the field, whether you are making a run out wide, behind the opposition's defense or dropping deep.

4.2 - Defensive Midfielders

The defensive midfielder is one of the most important positions in modern soccer as it provides extra cover for the defensive line and the position usually creates leaders on the field who can organize and instruct their teammates.

The defensive midfielder operates in the line between the defense and the center midfield, roaming laterally across this line to pressurize opponents when they are in possession and making tackles and interceptions to win the ball back. They are expected to win every duel in the center of the park, easing the pressure on their defense and staying tucked in behind the attacking line, collecting rebounds and miskicks so that they can restart the attack.

In possession, defensive midfielders must possess great ball handling skills, excellent decision-making skills, a deep knowledge of the game, and high levels of fitness. They will generally be the player that the defenders seek when they are in possession, so they must also have confidence in their ability with the ball at their feet and be able to pass the ball neatly and accurately.

Playing as a Defensive Midfielder

- Right Place Right Time

The key role performed by a defensive midfielder is to act as a barrier between the opponents and his or her defense. As such, a strong positional sense is a must. You may hear a commentator say 'so and so always seems to be in the right place at the right time', and there is a certain truth about that.

So how can you make sure that your positioning is how it should be? First things first, you must remember your role. Your starting position should be in the center of the field, and then you can engage the opposition before they have a chance to play that killer pass or get a shot away. So avoid getting dragged out wide to pick up a player UNLESS you are completely sure that you have sufficient cover in the area in front of the centerbacks.

There is a little less freedom for a defensive midfielder in an attacking sense, but you will be expected to recycle possession and pass the ball neatly to a player in a more advanced position, as well as offering an option to receive the ball too. But you won't want to be straying too far forward, as you will leave plenty of space in the middle of the park that could be exploited. Consider the middle third of the field as your territory, and you don't want anyone else to make their mark on it.

- Be Decisive

The defensive midfielder is the anchor of the team; the one that teammates will be looking to dominate the middle of the field, break up opposition attacks and start attacking advances of their own. So a decisive touch and a cool head are two key components for this role.

A well-timed tackle or a key interception can send confidence shooting through a team, and can be the platform on which meaningful forays forward are built on. As such, the most effective defensive midfielders are those that are happy to take on the burden as the spine of their team; the one that is looked upon to set the tone for a winning performance.

- Keep it Simple

All players have their own strengths and weaknesses, but the key role performed by defensive midfielders is to break up attacks and distribute the ball simply to a colleague. And that's the key to it; keeping things simple. It's no secret that this position on the field has been called the 'water carrier' before, and that refers to the perceived simplicity of the role. That's not to suggest it is an easy position to play, just that the tasks you need to perform must be kept to their most basic.

You may need to mark the opposition's playmaker and deprive him or her of the ball, but even that will come with a simple set of instructions. Get the ball, pass the ball – that is the defensive midfielder's modus operandi in a nutshell.

- Know your Opponent

Keep your friends close but your enemies closer, so the old saying goes. And that's true for the midfield battleground as well, where if you know your opponent's strengths and weaknesses you will have a fantastic advantage over them in the quest for midfield dominance. Being able to read your opponent like a book will enable you to anticipate their next move; which could allow you to intercept a pass or nick the ball off them and set your team on the offensive.

Do they have a good first touch? If they don't, you can stand off them a bit and wait for the second ball. If they do, you know you will need to close them down quicker. Maybe they favour one foot over the other? It makes sense then to show them onto their weaker side to minimise the chance of them making a dangerous contribution. Knowing your opponent's strengths and weaknesses will allow you to plan effectively and win the all-important midfield battle.

- The Team comes First

The role of the defensive midfielder is not always a glamorous one, but from a team perspective, its importance cannot be overstated. Very rarely will you get the glory – the great run and cross, the brilliant finish, the last ditch saving tackle, the fantastic save – but the work you will undertake on the field will go a long way to determining whether your team will win or lose a match. Your teammates will look to you as an integral cog in the machine, and whilst you may never get the headlines or the plaudits you will take great satisfaction from being the lynchpin of the team.

The role can also be seen as a 'helper': you're helping your defenders by acting as a screen in front of them and covering for them when they are out of position. You're helping your attacking colleagues by winning the ball from your opponents and setting them free. As such, the defensive midfielder can be defined as the ultimate team player – and the team should always come first. There may even be times when you have to commit a foul and perhaps take a booking, in the interests of the team. That is what you are there for, and your teammates will admire you endlessly for your selflessness.

- Make Yourself Available

As a deep-lying midfielder, you are likely to be in the privileged position of having plenty of space around you. As such, you should make yourself available to receive the ball from your teammates at all times. The attacking areas can often become congested, so help out your comrades by offering them the opportunity to recycle possession. Even if you move a couple of meters to your right or left, you are likely to be in a good position to receive the ball, but still in place to cover should your team's attack break down.

From your vantage point you are also in the privileged position of being able to see the whole game in front of you; so you should be communicating with your colleagues at all times as to which passes are on, when they are being closed down by an opponent – the classic 'man on' shout, and where the space is for your colleagues to run into. You will also need to call your attacking talents back when the opposition are breaking away.

Chapter 5

Defenders

Many people underappreciate the importance of a defender's job. Yet there is a strong argument that can be made for defenders being the most important position in soccer. They may not receive all the glory when they make a great challenge or break up an attack, but they are a vital clog in the functionality of a team.

The main reason defenders don't get as much credit as their teammates further up the field is probably due to the fact they rarely have a chance to get their feet on the ball and display skills, making their job less visually appealing than the attackers who create and score the goals.

Regardless of this, defenders form the backbone of a team, and a team with a strong defense, capable of routinely marking the fastest, toughest, and trickiest players, have a distinct advantage on the field.

A common phrase used when talking about defending is 'The Art of Defending'. This refers to the fact that defenders must follow several concepts to create a solid defensive line. It is all well and good having the skills and attributes required to be a defender such as tackling, jockeying, heading, etc. But if you don't follow the basics of defending you will find yourself out of position and struggling to keep pace with the match. Whether you are a center back or fullback, you should always follow these basic concepts:

- Stay Calm and Learn to Love the Ball

The modern defender is now expected to use the ball much more than was the case 10 – 20 years ago. A defender who shows panic when they receive the ball unsettles their teammates and is more likely to make a mistake.

It is important to stay as calm as possible when in possession of the ball, even if you are placed under pressure by the opposition forward, try to make a simple pass to a teammate, or if you are under severe pressure just kick the ball out to the flanks. Body language goes a long way in reassuring your teammates, and if you can ensure the people around you feel more confident and relaxed, your team will have a much better chance of winning the match.

- Be Aware of Your Surroundings

Part of staying calm and assured is knowing your surroundings on a field. If the ball comes to you, you should know exactly what's around you and where you are in relation to teammates, opposition players, and the sidelines. Similarly, when your team is out of possession, you should be gathering as much information as you can on what's going on around you. Use your eyes and ears to build up an almost radar-like picture of the play, allowing you to anticipate and communicate more effectively.

- Use your Strengths and the Opponent's Weaknesses

It goes without saying that your strengths may correlate nicely with your opponent's weaknesses. If you have been tasked with marking a small, nippy striker, then you can use your extra height and weight to bully them off of the ball. Of course, you don't want to give them an opportunity to use their pace, so keep them close and use your physical advantage to make sure they are kept quiet.

On the flipside, you could be a shorter defender who often has to mark attackers that are more physically dominant than you. Here you can use your strengths – agility, a burst of speed, low center of gravity – to nick the ball away from a larger opponent who perhaps doesn't possess the quickness of thought or feet that you do.

- Work as a Unit

Due to the offside rule, defenders must maintain their position on the field relative to the other players in the defensive line. This means being spread out along the backline, but not being too far from the midfielders in front or the defenders on the side. Listen to your goalkeeper, as they will have a better view of the game and be able to help you stay in line or mark an open opponent. Always be aware of where you are positioned in relation to the goal, your defensive teammates, and the midfielders ahead.

- Defending against Width

Teams that play wide can often be the toughest to defend against, as they utilise the whole width of the field to stretch even the most well-organized of defenses. This can lead to plenty of space for opponents to run into and exploit, so keeping in close proximity with the rest of your defensive unit is crucial.

If you are a fullback marking a winger, don't be tempted to hug the touchline and leave your center backs exposed. Instead, stay close to your center back and instruct a midfielder to help you deal with the wide player. Central defenders should hold their line and not be dragged out wide to cover their fullback – an optimum distance of around 7 - 12 meters between each defender is ideal. And don't forget to communicate with one another!

- Stay on your Feet

It doesn't matter whether an attacker is tall and strong or quick and fleet of foot, the basic tenets of defending remain the same. One of the most important of these is to try to stay on your feet at all times. A defender on the floor is of no use to their team, and with the success rate of sliding tackles being low, it is far more effective to play the percentages and attempt to shepherd your opponent away from goal or onto their weaker foot.

Classic Mistakes to Avoid

- Playing the Offside Trap at the Wrong Times

Executing an offside trap can be a brilliant way in which to catch an attacker or two in an offside position and halt a dangerous attack before it can become even more deadly for your team. But there are good times to attempt to play your opponents offside and there are bad times. Perhaps the worst scenario is when there is no pressure on the ball, i.e. the opposition midfielder has time to look up and pick his or her pass, as the attacker can simply time their run to perfection. In this case, you will want to drop deep to protect your defensive third of the field.

- Losing Sight of the Player you Should be Marking

As soon as you lose track of the player you are marking, your chances of stopping them scoring or creating chances greatly diminishes. The best way to mark is to keep your opponent slightly in front of you – close enough that you can keep tabs on them, but not too close so that they can spin you and sprint into the space behind.

- Letting Quick Players have Space to Run into

This is exactly what a player who relies on their pace wants: open space to run into. You should close them down as soon as possible to prevent them getting a yard or two away from you.

- Allowing Creative Players Time on the Ball

This is exactly what a creative player wants: time on the ball in order to pick out that killer pass. So again, get close to them and don't allow them the freedom to do as they please.

- Not Analysing your Opponent's Strengths

This is linked to the two points above: understanding the opponent you are dealing with is crucial. Try to identify their strengths as early as you can in a match – are they someone who relies on their pace, are they a skilful player, a playmaker, strong in the air, like playing with their back to goal, etc. By doing this, you can plan how to thwart them accordingly.

- Dropping too Deep

The temptation when playing against fast attackers with a creative playmaker pulling the strings is to drop deep to nullify the threat. But this can be deadly as it creates more space between your defensive line and midfield; offering new opportunities for the attacking team. Instead, keep a steady line and try to combat your opponents in different ways.

- Not Communicating with your Defensive Unit

So much of good defending is linked to communication. Letting your fellow defenders know when an attacker is lurking nearby, or when you seek cover, is crucial for remaining well organized and keeping your shape. Poor communication can be devastating; particularly with the fast pace of the modern game.

- Doing too Much with the Ball

In today's game, defenders ideally need to be comfortable in possession of the ball. But trying a trick to get past an opponent in your own penalty area is a step too far; you need to be avoiding danger to your goal at all times. So don't be tempted to try a skilful maneuver when an attacker is closing you down; sometimes the most effective form of defending is to remove the ball as far away as possible from your own goal.

5.1 - Center Backs

A center back (also known as a center half or a central defender) is tasked with defending the area directly in front of their own goal, attempting to prevent the opposing players, in particular the opposition's center forwards, from scoring a goal. A great center back is a key pillar in any successful side, possessing a great understanding of the position, bravery, and leadership qualities among many others.

When defending, central defenders use a broad range of skills such as blocking shots, tackling, intercepting passes, contesting headers and marking opposition players to discourage the opposing team from passing to them. But they must also possess basic ball skills and have the ability to make short and simple passes to their teammates or to kick long balls up field or to the flanks when clearing their area.

Teams usually deploy two or three center backs in front of the goalkeeper. These center backs must have an almost psychic understanding, knowing where the other is at all times and being able to cover their teammate if necessary.

There are many different combinations used by managers in an attempt to find the perfect partnership. Some managers play two big, physical players in the center back positions, some play one big player and one smaller, quicker player and some disregard physical appearance altogether and simply look for players with the right personality. Some of the best center back partnerships are reliant on personality over talent, although playing a dominant defender who is a ball winner beside a player with more finesse and composure is generally a winning formula.

Playing as a Center Back

- Use your Head

Whilst it's fair to say that soccer is played with the feet, so much of the game is acted out in the brain, and it tends to be the more intelligent players who seem to flourish. This is particularly true for center backs, who have to be able to read the game to an almost psychic degree in order to be one step ahead of the opposition. You need to be able to dictate their next move before they have even thought about it.

Soccer intelligence is like a normal IQ: it is largely naturally occurring, but you can improve your intellect by studying the subject. So take the time to watch your favourite defenders – their positioning, when they drop deep and when they engage their opponent in the tackle – and you will find that your own soccer IQ improves.

- Communicate! Communicate! Communicate!

It cannot be overstated how important good communication is for a center back and the overall success of their defensive line. A call at just the right time can alert a fellow defender to an opponent running into space, or lets them know you are covering behind once they commit to the tackle. A good offside trap is built around communication; letting your fellow defenders know when to step up. And a loud shout when the ball is played into your box can often put off an attacker and let them know that you are going to win the header at all costs.

- Be Brave

There are times as a center back where you will need to put your body on the line to protect your team's goal. Few particularly enjoy this aspect of the game, unless they are slightly unhinged, but in this way you can contribute so much to the team if you are willing to block a shot or put your head in where it might hurt. Take a look at Nemanja Vidic: when he played for Manchester United, he won his team so many points with his willingness to put his body on the line to stop goal-bound shots.

- Patience is a Virtue

There are times when a center back needs to be patient too; rather than charging in like a bull to a red rag. For example, if your opponent is slightly taller and slightly stronger than you, and the opposition play a long ball game, then you have to be patient and recognise that you might not win every header. Instead, you can read the game, anticipate where the opponent's flick on is going to go, and mop up the danger that way. Only fools rush in, as the old saying goes.

- The Center Back Partnership

As is often the case in soccer, the best players are elevated to new levels by the partnerships they create around them. It doesn't matter whether it is in defense, midfield or attack, developing an almost telepathic understanding with a partner will enable you to gain strength from one another and dominate your opponents.

This is particularly true for the center back partnership; the cornerstone of any successful team. You need to cover each other's backs, communicate well and work in tandem to ensure that your defensive line is impenetrable. The best partnerships are the ones in which the pair have clear defined roles – perhaps one is tasked with winning headers and stepping out to make tackles, and the other holds their position to cover and deal with any second balls. So get together with your central defensive partner and discuss each other's' strengths and weaknesses. From this, you should be able to assign key roles within the partnership to one another.

- Defending against a Target Player

This can be one of the trickiest skills to master for a center back. There are two general types of target player: the tall striker who wins a lot of balls in the air, and the strong attacker with good control who wants to receive the ball into feet before playing in a teammate. Defending against either of these is tough, so instead focus on two things: the opponent's first touch and the second ball.

Expect the target player to receive the ball, but make their first touch more difficult by giving them a nudge (without committing a foul) causing them to go slightly off balance, and then read where it will go from there. The number one rule of playing against a target player is to stop their supply in more dangerous areas of the field, so teamwork and solidity as a defensive unit will help in your mission to nullify their threat.

- Defending against a Quick & Nimble Striker

Defending against an especially fast striker has its difficulties too, especially if you play a flat back four. This creates plenty of space in behind, and it only takes a well-weighted through ball for you to be eating the attacker's dust. If you're playing in a back three, then the middle defender in the trio can act as a sweeper to cut off the supply. But in a back four, what you need to do is give yourself a bit of a headstart.

When you see a midfield opponent with the ball at their feet looking for a pass, just drop off slightly and create a few yards of space for yourself. The fast strikers who generally profit are those who play 'on the shoulder' of the last defender – so don't let them have that opportunity. You can always try to play an offside trap too, but be warned this takes plenty of practise, organisation and discipline: it is certainly not for the faint-hearted.

5.2 - Fullbacks

So many coaches prefer to field formations such as 4-3-3 or 4-3-2-1 to reflect the changing landscape of the game. Gone are the days of the standard 4-4-2, where defenders defended and attackers attacked. In these more fluid, modern systems, fullbacks need to contribute to all phases of play. The whole of the flank, from corner flag to corner flag, is now the fullback's domain, and they will be expected to be in position in both the defensive and attacking third.

As a consequence, they will need to be able to run all day and all night to get up and down the wing for 90 minutes, so a lot of stamina work will be needed on the training field. Timing of runs are vital too; as they could be left one-on-one with the opposing fullback if executed properly, giving ample opportunity to get to the by-line and square the ball across the face of goal, pull it back to the edge of the box or whip in a cross for the strikers to attack.

So honing attacking instincts, whilst doing the all-important defensive duties well is at the heart of being a good fullback. Chipping in with assists, key passes and – who knows – maybe even a few goals can make a fullback an integral part of the team. After all, they have key tasks to perform in defense and attack, and so the importance of a versatile fullback will not go unnoticed.

Playing as a Fullback

- Teamwork

Teamwork is, of course, at the heart of everything that a team can hope to achieve. Teams of 'individuals' will never reach the heights that they should, whilst eleven team players will pull together and strive to succeed – even when times are tough. Strong teamwork requires many different balls to be juggled, but perhaps the two most crucial ones are organisation and communication.

As a fullback, you will be expected to play your part in a solid defensive line, before bombing forward and being in the right place at the right time at the other end. Covering your center backs and supporting your winger are two ways in which you can contribute to the overall team aesthetic.

Top Tip:

✓ To keep a good team balance, it is best to only have one fullback going forward at a time. So if the right-back has gone into an attacking position, the left-back should drop into a defensive position, and vice versa.

- Positioning

You have to operate along the length of the field – and a full sized surface measures approximately 100 meters long! You're going to need to be able to cover large distances whilst still maintaining your positional sense. 'Right place at the right time' should be any fullback's motto.

Defensively, you need to maintain that compact shape, and support the center back on your left (if you are a right back) or right (if you are a left back). In an attacking sense, your position will largely be dictated by the pace of your team's build-up play: if you prefer quick moves then you'd better bomb on sharpish! But if you prefer slow build up then use your instinct to time your forward runs appropriately, and know when to hold your position and offer a simple outlet to keep possession.

As a fullback, you will also need to play a key role in the deployment of a successful offside trap; and positioning is once again a key requirement. You will need to step up in tandem with your fellow defenders when the call comes. Otherwise, you could be responsible for playing an opponent onside and leaving them with a clear path to goal. You will need to look along the defensive line and make sure you are always on the same wavelength as your teammates, because if you play too high a line then the winger will have plenty of space to get in behind, whilst if you are too deep then you will simply allow the attackers to break the defensive line without fear of being caught offside.

- Dealing with a Winger

The key to dealing with a winger is to quickly analyse the type of player they are and act accordingly. Are they a speedster that wants to go round you on the outside? Or do they want to cut inside on their stronger foot? When you have worked this out, then you can work on the techniques to combat their strengths. As a general rule of thumb, though, you need to show your winger away from goal – as ultimately that is what you are protecting – and block any cross/shot/pass that is forthcoming.

If you sense your winger has a weaker foot, then don't be afraid to 'invite' them on to it using your body shape and showing them space. If your winger is blessed with devastating pace, then you will need to either close them down just before they get the ball, or hang back a little and minimise the amount of space they have in behind you.

- Dealing with an Attacking Fullback

Managing the advances of an attacking fullback are the same as those listed above for dealing with your winger, but the obvious difference is that – sometimes – you might find yourself on the end of a two on one situation if your opponent's winger and fullback double up on you.

The key is to hold your line and hold your flank – don't be sucked into the ball as they can play a simple wall pass and expose the space you leave behind. You should call back your winger or bring across a midfielder to help level the playing field. Remember, you are defending your goal: that is the basic role of any fullback. So show the opposing fullback out wide and do your utmost to block any crosses that they attempt.

Chapter 6

Goalkeepers

The most specialized position on the field, a goalkeeper (often shortened to 'goalie' or just 'keeper') has the primary role of preventing the opposition from scoring a goal. During a match, goalkeepers can play a crucial role in organizing the team as they are the only players on the field with an unrestricted view of the entire field of play, providing them with a unique perspective on play development.

The role of goalkeepers has changed dramatically over the years, evolving due to new rules and systems of play. Initially, they had very limited mobility and stuck to their position between the posts, rarely venturing further than the six-yard box to catch an incoming cross or corner kick. However, in 1992, the International Football Association Board made changes to the laws of the game that affected goalkeepers dramatically, namely the back-pass rule.

During the days of back-passing, it was common for goalkeepers to drop the ball, dribble for a little bit, and then pick it up again when an opponent came closer, thus wasting prolonged periods of time, especially towards the end of matches. Therefore, a second rule was introduced at the same time as the back-pass rule which prohibits goalkeepers from handling the ball once they have released it for play and also allows the goalkeeper to hold onto the ball for a maximum of only six seconds.

These changes in the laws of the game have resulted in a generation of goalkeepers who play a much more active role in the team instead of just performing time-wasting routines. For this reason, almost every top level club employs a specialist goalkeeping coach who works solely with the goalkeepers in the squad.

In the modern game, a great goalkeeper can make or break a team, inspire a defense or make them panic on the ball, earn all the plaudits or receive all the blame. Their skill-sets can be broken down into three broad categories – mental, physical and technical. Every goalkeeper will have aspects from all these categories in differing ratios which will determine their style of goalkeeping and how they fit into certain tactics.

6.1 - Mental Attributes

Although physical and technical attributes are important, the mental aspect is what sets apart the good from the great. During a match, a keeper is required to perform various physical and technical moves such as precision passing, agile saves, and powerful leaps. But, the difference between success and failure in a performance can often come down to how mentally strong they are.

Every keeper is a bundle of contrasts when playing a match – anxious to make a save yet remaining in a relaxed state of mind to actually make the save. It is such contrasts that make them the toughest individuals to handle on the field. The ability to deal with success, failure, and pressure all within a 90 minute match is what ultimately determines their ability. A single mistake in an important match can destroy a goalkeeper's confidence and reputation, something no other individual player on the field has to deal with to such an extent.

The sort of pressure experienced by goalkeepers is certainly unique considering the fact that they are isolated in the penalty area with nowhere to run or hide. There are no tactical tweaks for them in the same way that an outfield player can be asked to change position or change role if they aren't performing well.

The best goalkeepers are slightly egotistical as they need to believe they are the very best at what they do. By truly believing they are the very best at what they do, they can assume the role of leader. Leadership in a keeper is all about gaining the trust of your defense, letting them know that you will always have their back and vice-versa. This can involve a lot of hard work on the training ground and by being consistent in movement and performance in matches. Every goalkeeper makes mistakes, but it is the ones who put their head up and go about fixing the mistake that will gain the trust of their defenders rather than the ones who look to blame someone else.

As well as leadership, the most important mental attributes for goalkeepers can be broken down as such:

Positioning

Being in the right place at the right time can make it seem like every attempt at the goal the opposition makes is coming straight towards you. This can impact mentally on the opposition forwards who will quickly become frustrated at their shots always finding the goalkeeper in the right place. On the opposite hand, poor positioning can leave vast areas of the goal for opposing forwards to aim at and make it much easier for them to score.

Positioning During a Match

This may seem obvious, but the key to great positioning is to always know where the goal is! If you watch a match, you may be surprised at how often the goalkeeper loses track of where their body is in relation to the goal, especially during a scramble in the penalty area or an event that distracts them temporarily. Knowing where your body is in relation to the goal posts will make sure that you can take up the optimum position and create the perfect angle for making the target as small as possible for the opposing forward. This can be achieved in three steps:

- The first step in doing this is to check the posts to make sure the starting position is ideal. Then whenever an opportunity arises in a match to divert your attention for a split second, check the posts again to confirm position is maintained in relation to the ball.

- The second step is to always try and position yourself on an imaginary line that runs from the center of the goal to the ball. This will make sure you can get to either post equally well.

- The third step is to make sure your position is far enough off the goal line to cover the angle created by the ball and both posts. This bit ties in with footwork as a goalkeeper should always be confident of covering either post with a couple of quick steps.

Following these three steps should guarantee that you always have the goal mouth covered and provide confidence that you won't be easily beaten with a shot from an opposing forward.

How to Improve Positioning

Positioning is something that is improved through hours of practice, both on the training field and during a competitive match. When working on your positioning in training, have your teammates shoot from various angles instead of all the shots coming from the center of the goal. If practicing with another goalkeeper, take turns in shooting from each side of the goal and from different positions each time. Before your teammate shoots, quickly check to make sure you are positioned in the correct angle facing the ball, an appropriate distance off your goal line, and that you can reach both posts in just a couple of quick steps.

Top Tips:

✓ Know the location of the goalposts at all times.

✓ Move far enough off the line to cover the angle of both posts.

✓ Be aware of being chipped or lobbed when coming off the line.

Reading the Game

Reading the game is an important part of being a soccer player, but even more so for a goalkeeper as they are the only ones who have a full view of the game being played in front of them. The ability to read the game ties in with a number of other attributes such as positioning, decision making, and confidence. A goalkeeper who can read the game well will naturally exude confidence in their ability, be more likely to make the correct decision, and will be able to naturally know where they should be positioned. When talking about reading the game, it can refer to a number of elements including tactics, timing, flow, and rhythm occurring in a match.

Reading the Game During a Match

One of the beautiful things about soccer is that it is such a fluid and complex game with any number of instances occurring that reading the game is a non-perfect act. It is impossible to tell exactly what will happen next while the game is in play. However, it is possible to use some basic decision formulas during a match to help read the game:

- Situation – This refers to both the positioning of the goalkeeper and the positioning of the ball. It is crucial to make sure that as a goalkeeper, you are in the correct position in relation to the ball and can anticipate a shot from distance or a through ball at any moment.

- Phase of Play – There are several phases of play established in matches – attacking, defending, the transition to attack, and the transition to defense. Goalkeepers should always be aware of what phase of play the match is in and act accordingly. For instance, if your team is in attack, it is likely going to be safe to wander further from your goal and act almost as a sweeper. But if your side is in transition to attack, there is a higher danger that a pass could be intercepted and a counter attack launched, so it is safer to stay closer to your goal. Therefore, knowing which phase of play the match is in can ensure you are always prepared.

- Rhythm of Possession – Some teams play with a certain rhythm of possession, holding onto the ball for long periods of the match in midfield trying to find a gap. Understanding both your team's rhythm of possession and your opposition's rhythm of possession can help you understand when an attack may occur.

Using these formulas combined can help you to read the game in a more accurate manner and therefore act appropriately. Remember, the goalkeeper is the only one who sees the full match in front of them and may need to communicate some of this information to their teammates.

How to Improve Reading the Game

Improving your reading of the game isn't something that can be practiced on the training field in the same way that footwork or positioning can be. The best way to improve it is by watching a lot of soccer with an analytical eye, keeping an eye on the phases of play, how the opposition is lining up, and what tactics are being employed. Use this information to imagine where you would be positioned if you were playing as the goalkeeper and how you would instruct your teammates. Another great way to improve your reading of the game is by making notes of passages of play you misread to learn from your mistakes.

Top Tips:

✓ Watch a lot of soccer matches with an analytical eye.

✓ Use the decision formulas – context, phase of play, and rhythm of possession to understand the game.

✓ Know the tactics of both your team and the opposition's team.

Reflexes

Having good reflexes allows a goalkeeper to make instinctive reaction saves and determines how well they can respond to the unpredictable with higher success, providing the ability to pull off saves for the highlight reel.

When a forward is firing in shots from close range through a packed penalty area, the goalkeeper needs to be on their toes and react quickly, particularly if the shot is deflected off a defender. It is impossible to predict what situations may occur in a match and therefore spending time practicing your reflexes on the training field is essential. There are several different methods that can be used to improve reflexes and prepare you for the unpredictable:

- Turn and Stop

This drill will help to develop recognition and reaction time. The drill begins with the goalkeeper standing facing the goal. The training partner will take shots, signaling just before striking the ball. The goalkeeper must then react quickly, turning around and attempting to make the save.

- Turn and Cover

A variation on the drill above, this one also begins with the goalkeeper facing the goal, but this time, the training partner will throw a ball at the goalkeeper's back. The goalkeeper must turn and cover the ball with their body as quickly as possible. In a match situation, a forward will be looking to pounce on any loose balls so the goalkeeper will only have a split second to react.

- Double Strike

This drill requires a goalkeeper to save two balls at the same time, improving both reflexes and decision making. The training partner will line up one ball a few meters in front of the goalkeeper and take a low shot with a second ball, aiming for the ball that is near the goalkeeper. If the ball is hit correctly, the goalkeeper will need to try and save whichever ball is on target. This recreates a match situation where a forward strikes a ball which is deflected off a defender or other player in the box.

- Drop Catches

In this drill, the goalkeeper and the training partner stand facing each other so they can reach and touch each other with outstretched arms. The training partner should hold a ball in each hand with their hands raised above their head. They then drop one of the balls while the goalkeeper tries to catch it before it hits the ground.

- Pick One

Sometimes goalkeepers attempt to predict where the ball will end up rather than using their reflexes. This tactic is never going to be 100% accurate, so using this drill can counter this instinct. Place two balls in the penalty area close together and have the training partner try to trick the goalkeeper by faking a shot and then shooting with the other ball. This drill helps decision making as well as reflexes.

Top Tips:

✓ Don't guess which direction a shot will take, instead watch the flight of the ball and react accordingly.

✓ Practice footwork, positioning, and decision making to make the most of your reflexes.

Communication & Command of Penalty Area

Communication is key for every player, but especially so for goalkeepers who are also in charge of commanding their penalty area. Once a goalkeeper has made a decision, the defenders need to know what it is so they can react appropriately.

Communication & Command of Penalty Area During a Match

You should have pre-arranged basic calls that let their defenders know quickly and efficiently what command to follow. The two most important calls are:

- **Keeper!**: This would indicate that the goalkeeper is coming to make a play on the ball whether that is catching it or punching it clear, and the defenders should move out of the way.

- **Away!**: This would indicate the opposite that the goalkeeper is not coming to collect the ball and the defenders should pursue it and try to clear it.

The goalkeeper must be able to yell these commands loudly and repeatedly if necessary. There can be no doubt in the mind of anyone whose ball that is during the split second. Any confusion can have disastrous consequences and lead to an opposing forward stealing the ball for a goal.

The goalkeeper should also direct traffic and position defenders on the field by knowing:

+ The defensive tactics employed by the team and how the coach wants the defenders to play.

+ The strengths and weaknesses of teammates and the opposing players.

+ The role of each defender and if they are fulfilling that role.

+ The ability to anticipate an attack by the opposition.

How to Improve Communication & Command of Penalty Area

Learning how to communicate and command your area as a goalkeeper is something that should gradually develop as a player matures. Goalkeepers generally need to have an outgoing and assertive personality to enable them to shout at defenders and yell commands.

One of the best ways to develop communication skills is to understand what, when, and how to communicate. The 'what' part of communication can be arranged with your teammates on the training field by coming up with a set of commands that everyone understands. However, the when and how is down to an individual and is something that only comes with lots of practice, playing in matches, and developing a deeper understanding of the game.

> **Top Tips:**
>
> ✓ Be loud and repetitive when commanding your area or communicating.
>
> ✓ Come up with a set of predetermined commands that everyone understands.
>
> ✓ Make sure you're aware of the tactics being employed and what is expected of your defenders.

Decision Making

Decision making for goalkeepers is absolutely critical as any decision a goalkeeper makes is final – there is no one behind a keeper to back them up if they make a mistake. Making the correct decision is about using a combination of other attributes such as reading the game, confidence, positioning, and even commanding your penalty area to make sure when you've made a decision to come for the ball everyone knows it!

Decision Making During a Match

It is very common that the first decision made by a goalkeeper when facing a shot is to not make a decision at all. Instead, you should react to a situation as it develops, rather than acting straight away, and should remain patient until the right moment comes. There are four rules of thumb that can help goalkeepers make the correct decisions:

1. Pressure the opposition's forward into making a decision. By placing the pressure on the forward, you are making them decide what to do. If a goalkeeper is well positioned and prepared, they won't need to act too soon.

2. Be prepared to pounce on a mistake. When an opposing forward makes a mistake, be ready to pounce on the ball and take charge of the moment.

3. Be ready to act as soon as the ball has been struck. Don't wait until the ball is mid-flight before being in the correct position and making the right decision. As soon as a ball has been shot or crossed, a goalkeeper should be prepared to spring in the correct direction.

4. Don't guess. If your positioning is right, you won't have to guess which way to dive and will be able to make the correct decision in a split second.

How to Improve Decision Making

Improving decision making is something that can be worked on during training. To do this, set up a drill with one goalkeeper, one forward, and five balls. The aim of the forward is to collect the balls one at a time, turn, and shoot. As soon as the forward has made a shot, they must sprint back to get the next ball and repeat as quickly as possible. The aim of the drill is for the goalkeeper to have to make snap decisions about angles, positioning, and which technique they will use to save the ball.

Top Tips:

✓ Always be prepared to allow you to make the best decision.

✓ Know which techniques are best for dealing with particular crosses and shots e.g. a very hard shot may be better if it's parried rather than caught.

✓ Have confidence in your decision making and apply decisions fully.

Confidence

Confidence is vital to any goalkeeper's mental attributes as it is one of the most psychologically challenging and demanding positions on the field. A mistake by a goalkeeper is always confidence-zapping, and the glory is generally reserved for the players at the other end of the field. Maintaining confidence is no easy task, especially if you've conceded lots of goals in a match or made a mistake that costs your team a victory. However, all goalkeepers must maintain a belief in their ability, keep their confidence high, and not let their heads drop.

Confidence During a Match/How to Maintain Confidence

In a match situation, goalkeepers react in many different ways after conceding a goal – some punch the floor, some shout and scream at themselves or their players, and some just get upset. It is very easy to let your head drop and become uninterested in the match after that third goal goes in, but as a goalkeeper, only you have the power to overcome adversity, improve your skills, and build your confidence back up. While maintaining confidence is all about personality and strength of character, it is always worth remembering:

+ Conceding goals happens: Goalkeepers want to save everything, but there are going to be goals that not even the best in the world could stop.

+ Focus on developing your skills: Don't place all your confidence in keeping a clean sheet, instead work on improving your game and your confidence will naturally grow.

+ Set realistic targets: If you want to improve your handling, don't set an unrealistic target of catching every ball, try instead to set realistic targets of gradual improvement.

+ Know what you did well: Even if you had a bad game remember the things you did well and be sure to give yourself high praise and acknowledgement.

+ Have support around you: When a goalkeeper wants to improve, their teammates should be offering all the encouragement and support they can. There's nothing that will restore confidence quicker than a teammate offering praise on improvements in your game or on something you did well.

6.2 - Physical & Technical Attributes

Technically speaking, a goalkeeper is still a soccer player, and soccer players are top-class athletes who are gauged on how much athleticism they possess. Unlike mental attributes, the physical and technical attributes can be measured quite accurately through training and skill tests.

The physique focuses on the aspects of a goalkeeper that are evident at first glance, many of which are due to genes and natural growth. Therefore, it stands to reason that some of these aspects can't be taught or attained on the training ground or in the gym, and are simply things a goalkeeper is born with. For example, height would be in this category as there is no amount of gym time that will help someone gain an extra two inches in height.

While it is not completely necessary, a tall goalkeeper is often seen as an advantage over a shorter one. The reason for this is that it is perceived that a tall goalkeeper with a reasonable height has a wider wingspan, a longer stride, and a higher vertical leap. Placing these together contributes to a goalkeeper's reach i.e. their ability to get to the ball and protect their goal area. This undeniably plays a huge part in making saves and catching the ball in the air from a cross or a corner, making them great shot-stoppers and reliable from set-pieces.

Speed is another of the most crucial physical attributes a goalkeeper can possess, as having the ability to react even only a millisecond quicker can provide the upper hand in many scenarios. In terms of reaction times and reflexes, it relates to how quickly a goalkeeper can spot an action (such as a shot at goal, a pass that sets up a goal scoring situation, or a cross into the box) and react accordingly. They must also possess quick feet and be able to use their footwork in a range of scenarios including running up and into a dive, coming off the line to narrow the angle for a forward, and so on.

The most important technical attributes can be broken down as follows:

Handling

The only advantage a goalkeeper has over any other player is the ability to use their hands. In this way, a goalkeeper can control the ball in a unique way, although in order to gain control they must possess great handling abilities. Handling refers to how securely the goalkeeper holds on to the ball when making a save or coming for a loose ball, essentially how well they can catch the ball. A keeper with good handling is less likely to give up rebounds to the opposition or to let the ball slip in bad weather.

Basic Types of Catches

There are several types of catches that can be used including:

- The 'W' or Contour Catch

This catch is used for any ball that arrives from around waist height up. As you catch the ball, your thumbs and index fingers should form a 'W', hence the name. It is vital that the hands, and in particular the thumbs, are behind the ball when making this type of catch otherwise the ball could slip through the grip and bounce into the goal or rebound to an opponent.

- The Inverted Contour

This catch is used for balls that arrive below the waist, with one hand positioned directly behind the ball, but this time facing downwards with both pinky fingers and palms used to control and make the ball safe. For very hard, low shots, your weight should be over the ball and your momentum should be forward and not static or backwards.

- Ground or Rolling Ball Pickup

There are several techniques that can be used to pick up a rolling ball, all of which involve getting your hands all the way down with your fingertips brushing the ground for a clean catch. The three styles of ground or rolling ball pickup are: Straight-leg pickup, knee-bent pickup, and knee-down pickup. All three of these techniques are acceptable, and it is simply a matter of using the technique that is most appropriate at the time and the one in which you feel most comfortable performing.

Protecting the Ball After a Catch

Making a catch is just the first part of handling, as you need to make sure you hold on to the ball afterwards so as to not give away an easy rebound to an opposition forward. The proper position for protecting a ball after a catch features both forearms vertical with hands curled over the top of the ball. In this position, it is almost impossible to dislodge the ball or to let it slip.

Be sure not to attempt to protect the ball too soon after a catch as this can lead to it bobbling out of your arms or ricocheting off your chest. Wait for the ball to settle in your arms after catching it before moving it gently into the protection position.

How to Improve Handling

As with any technical skill, to improve handling you must put in hours of practice. During training there are sure to be plenty of drills where teammates are taking shots on the goal which will allow you to work on handling. But it is also possible to practice your handling skills using just a ball and a wall. By kicking the ball off the wall from different positions and at different heights and trying to catch it and protect it, you can work on your handling skills as well as your reflexes and positioning.

Top Tips:

✓ Always have both hands fully behind the ball.

✓ When catching the ball, keep your body behind the ball to give you extra security,

✓ Try to always catch the top half of the ball, because if you're unable to control the ball it should drop to the ground in front of you.

Shot Stopping

There are occasions when a goalkeeper won't be able to catch the ball and use their handling skills, but of course it must still be prevented from going into the net. This skill is known as shot stopping – the ability of a goalkeeper to get in the way of and block incoming shots. The best goalkeepers are able to judge the flight of the ball and adjust their bodies accordingly to stop swerving or powerful shots. The best way of doing this is by Parrying.

Parrying

Occasionally a ball may be too far away to catch cleanly, but just a fingertip can be enough to send the ball high or wide. Parrying is the technique that is used to achieve this. Using the open hand (this could be the palm of the hand or the fingertip depending on the save), a goalkeeper should redirect the ball. Extended fingers have a few more inches of reach than a closed fist in addition to having more control over the redirection of the ball.

- High Balls

When parrying a high ball, you must quickly decide which side the ball is going to, move your hips into the correct position, and use a crossover step to move backwards as quickly as possible. As the flight of ball reaches the optimum position, leap upwards and slightly backwards, using the opposite side hand to get to the ball (for instance if the ball is on the left side use the right hand). Use the fingertips and top of the palm to direct the ball straight up as the momentum of the ball will likely see it over the top of the crossbar.

- Low Balls

When a low ball is coming in at pace and is slightly too far out of reach for a catch, you can parry it around the post. When using this technique, use the hand that is closest to the ball, usually the bottom hand when diving. When parrying low balls, use good footwork to get into the correct position for a dive, explode through the ball and lead with the hand closest to the ball. The heel of the palm should be used in this technique to achieve maximum power in the deflection while maintaining an element of control.

Top Tips:

✓ For low shots, if you are able to reach the ball with the other hand, position it on top of the ball for maximum security.

✓ Always parry to the sides of the goal and away from the strikers.

Punching

Punching is mostly used when the ball has been crossed into the box and the keeper has deemed it not safe enough to catch, usually because of a crowded penalty area or a striker lurking nearby.

Although punching can be risky as you have less control over where the ball will end up and are using a smaller surface area to hit the ball with, at times it is the better option and with a good technique, it can be a very effective way of clearing the danger. There are three keys to an effective punch:

- **Width** – Getting the ball towards the sidelines and away from the center of the field.

- **Distance** – Getting the ball as far away from the goal as possible.

- **Height** – Getting the ball over the opposition's forward players.

The proper hand position for punching is important for the best control and avoiding injuries to your fingers. The hands should form a fist, with the four fingers forming a flat surface and the thumb pressed firmly against the side of the fist but below the flat surface and out of harm's way. Punching can be achieved with one or both hands. If you want the ball to go back in the direction it's coming from, use two hands. If you want the ball to continue away in the same direction, use one hand.

Top Tips:

✓ When coming to punch the ball, always give a shout letting everyone know you intend to come for the ball.

✓ Aim to get the ball as far away from the center of the penalty area as possible.

One-on-Ones

A one-on-one situation requires all the skills that a goalkeeper can muster – technique, timing, bravery, and courage. A successful save in a one-on-one has the potential to turn the tide of a game and provide a lift to the whole team, but in order to make the save a goalkeeper must have a solid technical foundation. Proper technique also serves to prevent injury in what is a potentially dangerous situation.

There are three main components to a one-on-one situation:

- Positioning

A proper starting position is important since poor positioning can leave the goalkeeper stranded in no man's land or leave the goal wide open for the opposition striker. As the opponent is bringing the ball towards goal, you should start creeping forwards in order to cover more of the goal. The further off your line you go, the more you have to force your opponent out wide which might give you more time and can sometimes allow your defenders to get back.

Once you find yourself up against your opponent, try to steady yourself, stay on your feet, stay low, and make yourself as big as possible. If your opponent decides to shoot, the better your positioning and reactions are, the more likely you will be able to make a save. If your opponent decides to dribble around you, try to force them to the side you want them to go to, and if timed correctly you might be able to snatch the ball from their feet.

- Timing

A perfectly executed save at the wrong time can make a goalkeeper look foolish, but a well-timed attempt, even without perfect technique, provides a great chance of stopping the forward. There are several keys to timing a save in a one-on-one situation:

Time the forward. Be ready to charge the second the forward makes a mistake. Wait for them to make a long touch and try to get to the ball when it as far from the forward's foot as possible. Barring that, you should attempt to make a challenge just as the forward touches the ball so that you can get there before they take another touch.

Match the forward's pace. If the forward is coming in slowly, you should also approach slowly, with the same applying if the forward is coming in quickly.

Once committed, don't stop. When you have made a decision to go to ground or make a challenge, commit fully to the decision and don't second guess yourself.

- The Sliding Save

The sliding save is used when you attempt to snatch the ball from the forward's feet. To begin, approach the forward in a slightly modified position with your hands close to the ground. When the moment is right, begin to slide with your feet towards the center of the goal and your body square to the forward and centered so that the ball is around your lower chest or midsection. Finally, smother the ball with your hands before the forward has a chance to touch it again and hook both hands over the ball for maximum protection.

Top Tips:

✓ Once you commit to coming out of your goal, there is no going back.

✓ Stay on your feet for as long as possible.

✓ Approach in a low and ready position, and make yourself as big as possible.

✓ Only perform the sliding save as a last resort.

✓ Get your hands on the ball first when making a sliding save.

Ball Distribution

Although the goalkeeper is the last line of defense, they are also the first line of attack, especially in the case of a sweeper keeper. After a save is made or after a back pass from a defender, a quick restart or pass can be very effective in creating an attacking opportunity for your team. Ball distribution can be done in two ways: kicking the ball and throwing the ball. Both have advantages in different situations during a match.

Kicking the Ball

A goalkeeper can kick the ball in several ways – by dropping the ball and taking a normal kick, by punting the ball, by drop kicking the ball, or a simple short pass to a teammate. For maximum distance, a punt is usually the best option, but due to the high trajectory of the ball it generally ends up in a 50-50 situation at the receiving end.

When punting the ball, take a short run up at a slight angle to the kicking direction with the planted foot aiming towards the target. Drop the ball (don't toss it upwards!) and kick, following through to land on the kicking foot.

A drop kick provides slightly less distance but with a lower trajectory and is a better option for driving the ball into the wind. The technique is similar to a punt, except the kick is timed so the foot strikes the ball just after it bounces on the ground.

Throwing the Ball

Throws are generally much shorter than kicks, though they provide much more accuracy. A quick throw to the feet of an open teammate is the safest form of distribution, with several different throws available including:

- Roll

The roll is the most accurate but also the shortest form of distribution. Control the ball with the palm of the hand and the forearm with a bent wrist, step with the opposite foot, and 'bowl' the ball ensuring the fingertips touch the ground on delivery. This will require bent knees and a low waist.

- Javelin Throw

In the center of the accuracy and distance scale is the javelin throw, named so because it is similar to how a javelin is thrown. The ball starts in the palm of the hand beside the head and is thrown straight forward as you step into the throw. Placing backspin on the ball will make it easier to receive so let the ball roll off your fingertips slightly at the end of the release.

- Sidearm Throw

In terms of distance and accuracy, the sidearm throw is very similar to the javelin throw. The only difference is in its delivery - it is easier for the receiver to control the ball as the bounce of the ball will be lower. This throw involves extending the arm back slightly behind the body at a three-quarter angle, not straight to the side but just below shoulder level. The ball is then delivered with a slinging, swinging motion. Due to the arm position being sideways, the best way to place backspin on the throw is by passing the palm of the hand under the ball upon release.

- Overhand Throw

The overhand throw is the longest in terms of distance but also the least accurate. The ball is controlled between the palm and the forearm with a bent wrist. Point your non-throwing arm in the air straight ahead of you at a 45 degree angle and place your throwing arm behind you. Throw the ball by slinging your throwing arm over your head and bringing your non-throwing arm down. Make sure that both elbows remain locked. Also, just before you throw the ball, take two steps forwards to provide extra momentum.

How to Improve Distribution

Distribution is an area that can be worked on with the rest of the team when they are practicing passing and accuracy. However, it is important to practice both throwing and kicking and as such there are drills that can be set up specifically for goalkeepers. One such drill is to place targets in various positions around a soccer field, covering all areas of the field from the wing to the middle and from close to the goal to past the halfway line. The aim is to try and hit the targets which are closest by throwing the ball and the targets which are furthest away by kicking the ball.

Top Tips:

✓ When kicking, make sure the plant foot is facing the target.

✓ If kicking a long ball up field, aim for a teammate who is most likely to win a 50/50 duel.

✓ When throwing, roll fingers under the ball to provide backspin.

✓ Make sure throws have a low trajectory, ideally hitting the ground before they reach the receiver.

Chapter 7

Set-Pieces

A good set piece routine offers a fantastic opportunity for your team to score when carried out correctly. It is estimated that around 30% of the goals scored each season in the English Premier League come from set pieces; so you can see the potential in practising your own set plays and what it can bring to the team.

Professional clubs spend hours practising their set piece routines – both attacking and defending – to make sure they have another string to their bow. Some players, like David Beckham, would also spend hours of their own time after training practising their technique and delivery.

Remember, you may only get one chance and one chance alone to make a set piece count. It could be the difference between scoring/conceding a late goal or not, and so your execution needs to be spot on. There is no margin for error, therefore every player in your team needs to know their role in the routine and must be confident of executing this when the time comes.

There are four main types of set pieces to consider:

- Free Kicks

- Corners

- Penalties

- Throw Ins

Set Piece Success

All players will have a designated role within a set piece – even for penalties, where they are likely to be the taker, awaiting a rebound from the goalkeeper on the edge of the penalty area or back defending on the halfway line.

This is particularly true for corners and free kicks, where your coach may have devised routines to deploy in a match situation. You may be delivering the set piece, you may be tasked with undertaking a decoy run or you might be expected to get on the end of the delivery. Whatever your role, make sure you are confident in your own execution with plenty of practice.

There are, generally speaking, three measures of success for any set piece:

- ✓ Planning and preparation

- ✓ Accurate delivery

- ✓ Effective movement in the target area (crosses and free kicks)

If all three of these components are handled correctly, then your team could well add a dozen or more goals to their armoury each season.

7.1 - Free Kicks

A free kick is awarded when a player infringes the rules of the game in one way or another. It could be for a foul, handball or obstruction, and – if within a suitable range – offers an opportunity for a shot or cross to be delivered.

Remember, there are two types of free kick: direct and indirect. With a direct free kick, you can strike the ball and score without the ball needing to touch another player. These are awarded for offences as listed below, and if they are committed in the 18 yard box then a penalty is given.

Direct free kicks are awarded for:

- Foul

- Handball

- Violent conduct

An indirect free kick means that the ball needs to touch another player before crossing the goal line, otherwise the goal cannot be given. An example would be a cross into the box, one player tapping the dead ball to another to shoot, or firing the ball into a crowded penalty area and hoping for a deflection into the net.

A penalty will not be awarded should an indirect offence take place in the 18 yard box; instead the indirect free kick must be taken from where the incident took place.

Indirect free kicks are awarded for:

- Obstruction

- A goalkeeper handling a pass back or throw in

- A goalkeeper holding the ball for more than 6 seconds

Shooting

(You might want to refer back to chapter 1.2)

So many goals are scored each and every weekend by well-practised players curling, blasting or placing the ball into the net direct from a free kick. If the offence is committed within 30 meters of goal and in either a central or slightly off-central position, then your first thought should be to shoot for goal.

First things first, you should take a few sample free kicks on the training ground to see if you have a natural aptitude for it. Set the ball up in various locations around the penalty area, and create a makeshift defensive wall out of anything reasonably tall that you can find – trash cans are a good example, and set these up 10 meters away from the ball. If you can get some human volunteers to form a wall then even better!

Think about where you want the ball to go when you shoot. More importantly, think about where your shot will be the hardest to save – goalkeepers never enjoy it when the ball is struck right into the top corners of the goal. Watch any past free kick master and that is exactly where they aim.

Generally, there are two types of free kicks that you can take: placement or blasting the ball.

To place a free kick, you want to be getting it as close to the top corner of the net as possible – ideally on the side of the goal where the goalkeeper isn't stationed. The best technique to accomplish this is to strike the ball with your instep (the inside of your foot) just below the center of the ball, and slightly lean back. This will enable you to elevate the ball over the defensive wall and get the requisite height to hit the top corners.

Your follow-through, the angle of your foot when striking the ball, and how far to the right of the ball you can hit it (if you are right-footed) will determine how much bend you can achieve. It's a tough skill to master, but one worth persevering with. Two of the finest 'placement' free kick takers to play the game are David Beckham and Andrea Pirlo. To get yourself acquainted, search for some of their finest work on YouTube.

To blast a free kick, it is all about technique and timing. This is perhaps a harder skill to pull off then placing a shot as less accuracy is involved: you simply want to beat the goalkeeper with sheer power.

The technique is still important though: you need to be striking the ball in the center (or just to the side) with the laces of your boots, and leaning slightly forward so as not to send the ball sky-high. This way you can achieve maximum power whilst still getting the elevation required to maneuver the ball over the wall. When struck correctly, the ball will travel at speed and hopefully deviate in the air slightly, deceiving the goalkeeper.

Perhaps the finest 'blaster' of free kicks was the legendary Brazilian Roberto Carlos, so hunt down his best videos on YouTube and acquaint yourself with the work of a master.

Arguably the greatest free kick taker of all time, Juninho Pernambucano developed a clever fusion of placement and power. Although an extremely difficult technique to master, it is definitely worth checking out some of his videos.

Practising Shooting Free Kicks

The key to perfecting your free kicks is to practise as regularly as possible. It can be hard with your other training needs and, not to mention, having a personal life, but do try to practise striking the ball at least once a week if you are serious about becoming your team's designated set piece taker.

Believe it or not, practise isn't just about placing or blasting the ball where you want it to go. It's about confidence: the confidence created by knowing that when that one chance comes in a real match, you will be ready to take it. Practice also creates repetition, and repetition is important in recreating a consistent strike of the ball each and every time.

Watch some of the top free kick takers in the world just before they hit a free kick. They enter an almost zen-like state, where they look at the ball, then at where they want to hit it, and then back at the ball again. This is them visualising where they want the ball to go (the top corner would be nice!) and how they will achieve it. Get into the habit of taking a moment to replicate this – even just in practise.

And remember, once you have made your mind up where you are going to hit the ball simply relax your body and go for it: no holding back. At first, you may find yourself sending the ball miles wide or over. This is okay; it is just part of the learning process. With repetition, you WILL get better.

So get out onto the training field or down your local park, take as many soccer balls as you can carry, and practise striking a dead ball. Once you are more advanced and confident in your technique, introduce fun challenges – like hanging an old tin can or piece of fruit from the cross bar with a piece of string, and practise hitting it. Start with a big object, then slowly decrease in size, and you will notice your accuracy improving.

> **Top Tips:**
>
> ✓ If you want to create topspin on the ball, use the instep of your foot and hit the ball at a low point. As soon as your foot has connected with the ball, bring your foot up over the top. This is useful for dipping the ball over the opponent's wall.
>
> ✓ Focus and mental toughness are part of striking the perfect free-kick. Try to shut out everything around you and concentrate on your technique.

Crossing

A slightly different art to shooting from a free kick, but in its own way no less important is crossing. When an infringement is committed on the field in a position which is not receptive to a direct shot, e.g. out wide by the touchline, then a good delivery into the penalty area is another method of creating (hopefully) a goal-scoring opportunity.

What will typically happen is that a mini defensive wall will be set up in front of you to prevent your cross from entering the penalty area. In the box will be a selection of players: your teammates being marked by your opponents.

It is likely that your coach will instruct your tallest players to stand in the most dangerous position (on or around the penalty spot). Your smaller players will then make a series of runs in an attempt to shake off their markers and to confuse those marking your tall players and those that are strong in the air with good heading ability.

Your mission will be to deliver the ball either to a pre-determined target (your coach will have instructed you who on the training field) or into a dangerous area, with the ultimate aim of creating an opportunity to score.

The Technique

The technique for delivering a good cross from a free kick into the box is much the same as that of shooting from a free kick. Make sure you have a long look at your target before preparing your delivery – visualisation is very important. Imagine in your mind the ball going exactly where you want it to.

You then need to decide which type of ball you want to send into the box: a floated cross or a whipped ball. The floated cross is designed for the taller players in the team – this will enable them to take advantage of their extra height. The whipped ball is better when you don't have any particularly tall players; instead it relies on the accuracy of the cross and the finishing prowess of the target.

For the floated cross, place your non kicking foot slightly behind and to the side of the ball. If you are right footed this will mean putting your left foot slightly behind and to the side of the ball, and vice versa for left-footed players. Strike the ball with your instep at the bottom of the ball, using a slow and smooth action, and lean back a little. This will generate the elevation required to send the delivery into the box at a decent height.

For the whipped ball, address the ball with your non kicking foot in the same way described above. When striking, again use the instep of your foot, but this time hit a slighter higher contact point on the ball – just below center. You should aim to strike the ball faster and with more 'whip', so hit through the ball quickly and follow through.

Danger Zone Crossing

As a defender, one of the worst situations you have to face is danger zone crossing from a free kick. Danger zone crossing is when a ball is played between the line of defenders and the goalkeeper, usually between a yard before the penalty spot and a yard before the 6 yard box (as shown in the diagram below).

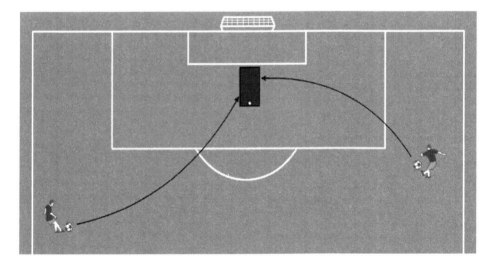

If the ball is crossed into the area shaded above, whether it be ground or head height, it can be very difficult for defenders to clear the ball and for goalkeepers to come out to catch or punch the ball. Simply put, it's a nightmare to defend against!

If you are the free kick taker in your team, and you have a free kick in a good position out wide, the ultimate test of your opponents' defensive capabilities will be from danger zone crossing.

A good delivery could result in one of your teammates getting an easy header on goal, or maybe the goalkeeper comes out and totally misses the ball, leaving an open goal. Perhaps a defender running back accidently scores an own goal, maybe even everybody misses the ball and your free kick ends up in the corner of the net. This is what makes danger zone crossing so dangerous, the fact that there are so many ways for the ball to go into the back if the net.

Practising Crossing Free Kicks

As ever, practising your skill set leads to repetition, and repetition is the best possible preparation for the match situation. So get out on the training ground with a bunch of soccer balls and get crossing. You can enhance your practice by placing inanimate objects in the penalty area as pretend targets. As you improve, make these targets smaller and harder to hit.

If you can politely ask for some human volunteers to replicate the common movements in the penalty area just prior to a set piece then great, as this will help you to focus while chaos is ensuing around your target.

Top Tip:

✓ When danger zone crossing, try to have a right footer take the free kick on the left side of the field, and a left footer on the right. This way, if nobody makes contact with the ball there is a slight chance it could sneak its way into the corner of the goal.

7.2 - Corners

Corners are one of the most common and perhaps the most important set piece for any team. It enables you to get a free cross into the box and aim it at your desired target – a tall teammate or a dangerous area, for example. With so many goals coming from corners, you need to be well prepared to defend and attack crosses as they come in.

Tactically, you want your tallest players and those with great heading ability in the key areas of the penalty area: the penalty spot and along the six-yard line. This is where they are at their most dangerous in an attacking sense and their most effective defensively. Then, smaller players can dovetail around them, make runs to act as a decoy and generally make a nuisance of themselves.

Sometimes, your team or your opponents may opt to play a 'short' corner. Here, a player will stand within a meter or so of the corner taker, receive the ball and then deliver it into the penalty area. The reason for this is that the crosser can create unique trajectories from this slightly less acute angle.

Attacking Corners

The most important aspect of an attacking corner is the delivery. A good ball can make magic happen; a bad ball will undo any strategies you have worked on during training. If you are tasked with delivering a corner, make sure you follow the tips outlined in the 'free kicks' section of this chapter.

If you are stationed in the penalty area, then you will need to decide whether you plan to attack the ball or simply make a nuisance of yourself. If you are tall, a good jumper or have decent heading ability, you want to station yourself on or around the penalty spot and wait for a good delivery to head towards goal. If you are none of these things, then you can still get involved: you can make a run for the near post or lurk at the back post in case the cross is mis-hit, or you can stand by the goalkeeper and make his or her life a misery!

The biggest annoyance to a defender at set pieces is movement. Never stand still for a second: it makes you too easy to mark. Stay on your toes, and keep darting around the penalty area. You may be able to lose your marker, and should the ball fall to you then you might have a free shot at goal.

A position that players with good ball control and shooting ability like to take up at corners is just outside the penalty area. That way, if the opponents win the header or the goalkeeper punches the ball clear, the ball might land at their feet and they will be able to fire a long range shot at goal.

Always be prepared for ricochets and 'second balls' once the corner has been delivered. It's amazing how many crosses into the box cause confusion and panic amongst even the most assured defensive units. Never switch off and assume the chance has gone because you never know when a golden opportunity might come your way.

And practise, practise, practise your finishing and heading. On the training field you hone your skills to be ready for the match, so taking the time to work on your finishing when there is no pressure on is vital. Recreate corner situations with your teammates and get somebody to load crosses into the box. This will help you to work on finishing half chances and timing your leap to head the ball.

Top Tips:

✓ Position yourself in the box relative to your strengths.

✓ Stay on the move to avoid easy marking.

✓ Be prepared for anything – ricochets, deflections and 'second balls'.

Defending Corners

Defending your goal from corners can be simple or more complex depending on your coach's preferred strategy. The most popular way is man marking, where you will be asked to mark an opponent that is a similar size and build to yourself. Here the responsibility is on you individually to make sure your opponent doesn't get a header or shot on goal.

This is a great system where the two teams are similarly matched physically, as it will give you and your teammates a good shot at winning the vast majority of headers. But if your team is shorter and weaker than your opponents then a zonal system might be right for you.

Zonal marking can be a more complex strategy for defending corners. Imagine the penalty box as a chessboard, split into small squares. In a zonal marking system, you will be given a number of these connected squares to 'guard'. It could be a channel at the front or back post, along the six-yard line or penalty spot, or awaiting onrushing attackers from the edge of the box. The responsibility thus becomes a collective one, although you are in sole charge of your particular zone.

The idea behind zonal marking is that the attackers' movements can be unpredictable, and so it removes the risk of defenders losing track of who they are supposed to be marking. With zonal marking, this problem is allayed in the knowledge that each zone of the penalty area is taken care of. Players cannot be dragged out of position by their targets.

But the system has its critics too. Defenders can be left flat-footed and stood still in their zones, which means that an onrushing attacker can usually jump higher than them due to their momentum.

The zonal marking system can only be effective if defenders are alert to danger, are able to leap from a standing position well, and each player knows their responsibilities inside out.

Top Tip:

✓ Some coaches like to put defenders on the post. If you find yourself in this position, as soon as the ball has been cleared from your penalty area sprint off your post until you are in line with your defensive line. As you would be the last defender, you could be playing many of your opponents onside; therefore it is vital that you get back to your team's defensive line as soon as possible.

7.3 - Penalties

An infringement that would otherwise lead to a direct free kick if the incident takes place outside of the penalty area is punishable with a penalty if it occurs inside the box. This gives an attacker a free shot at goal from 12 yards, with just the goalkeeper to beat.

As such, a penalty is the most sought-after set piece, with statistics estimating that around 85% of penalties end with a goal being scored. It could be the best chance you get to score in a match, so it makes sense to make sure you are ready when the opportunity comes.

There are numerous ways to approach a spot kick. Some players will simply run up to the ball and blast it as hard as they can – hoping that the speed of their shot is greater than the reaction speed of the goalkeeper.

Some will pick a side of the goal to aim at and shoot with their side foot; aiming for precision and placement rather than power. If executed correctly, the ball will nestle in the corner of the net with the keeper given no chance.

Some will try to out-fox the goalkeeper by waiting for their movement. These cheeky players will run up to the ball and stutter midway through, all in the hope that the keeper will move to one side or the other.

Some will make their minds up simply to shoot down the middle of the goal no matter what, and hope that the keeper has already made their mind up to dive to one side.

The issue is made somewhat cloudier by the actions of the goalkeeper. Some will just pick a corner to dive towards and hope for the best, while others will wait and see if they can determine anything from the taker's demeanour or movement as to what they plan to do.

How to Take the Perfect Penalty

Of course, if there was no pressure involved you would probably fancy yourself to score maybe eight or nine times out of ten from the spot. But really, the added pressure of the match situation makes the job much harder.

Remember, the goalkeeper is always a hero if they save the kick, whilst the taker is cast as a villain if they miss. Should they score nobody bats an eyelid, because really you should score a penalty.

So now you can see the pressure that a penalty kick creates. Hopefully that hasn't put you off! Here are some little tips and pointers:

- Pick a Side – and Stick With It

The worst thing you can do is change your mind halfway through your approach to the ball. Try to plan ahead of time whether you want to place or blast the ball, and to which side (or even down the middle if you're feeling confident), and let fate deal with the rest.

- Technique and Concentration are Key

A tactic the opposition (especially the goalkeeper) might employ is to try to distract you. They might come to talk to you pre-shot, make unusual movements, or try to delay your penalty kick for as long as they can. The best way to counter this is to place the ball on the penalty spot as soon as you can, measure your run-up, and just stare at the ball until the referee allows you to take the penalty. Staring at the ball allows you to drown out all distractions and focus on how and where you strike the ball.

- Don't Over-Think it

At the end of the day, it is just you, a goalkeeper, a ball, a goal and 12 yards separating you. All things considered, it really is as simple an equation as that. If you are well practised and confident and strike the ball cleanly, you should score. There really is no need to over-complicate matters with feints, chips or body swerves.

- Practise!

The more you practise, the more comfortable you will feel. Even when the pressure is on, if you have been striking your penalties well in training then you will feel a lot more confident. It is impossible to recreate the pressures of a match situation in a relaxed surrounding, so instead raise the stakes in practise against your teammates – have a shoot-out and state that the loser has to buy the winner dinner, or has to perform some kind of forfeit!

7.4 - Throw-Ins

To the casual observer, a throw-in would seem like the perfect opportunity to take a breather from the frenetic pace of the game. But nothing could be further from the truth: many teams use throw-ins as the perfect time to launch their next attack; whether whey opt to throw it short and keep possession, or heave it long into the opponent's penalty area.

Throw-ins are generally taken by the either the fullback or winger on the side of the field where the ball went out of play, although if a quick throw-in offers an opportunity for a slick attack then whoever is nearest will take the throw. If your team possesses a long throw specialist amongst its ranks, and the ball goes out of play within easy reach of the opponent's penalty area, then they will take over responsibility.

The object, of course, is to find a teammate with your throw, but there are two ways you can do this: with a short throw or a long throw.

A short throw gets the ball back in play and ensures your team keeps possession in a low risk way. A long throw, if the ball is in the right hands, can become like a cross in its own right, and this naturally can lead to goal-scoring opportunities.

The Technique

To remain 'lawful', and not get flagged up for a foul throw, both of your feet must remain flat on the ground at all times when taking the throw. The ball must be held in both hands behind your head, and then released with a straightening of the arms.

Anything other than this – throwing the ball with bent arms, with one arm, or with one foot in the air – will result in a foul throw being awarded. This grants possession of the ball to the opposing team.

It is possible to perform a kind of run-up prior to throwing the ball in, which helps to generate velocity and distance, but you must adhere to the rules outlined above.

Short Throw-Ins

A short throw-in is simply an exercise in retaining possession and getting the ball back into play. If you are the taker, then you will be looking for options close at hand who have broken free from their marker with a timely run. Your teammate will then control the ball and lay it off, or return it to you first time – so don't switch off and lose focus once you have thrown the ball back into play.

If you are in the vicinity of the throw-in, make sure you make yourself available to receive the ball. Good movement is key, as this will enable you to lose your marker and find some space. A clever practise for this skill is to mark out a small area in cones on the training field and play a game of 'flag soccer' – where you have a training vest tucked into the back of your shorts and your teammates must try and get it from you, whilst you evade capture.

Once the ball has been thrown to you, a good first touch will help you to bring the ball under control and buy you some time to pick out your next pass.

Long Throw-Ins

A long throw can be a devastating attacking ploy. This is akin to a corner of free kick delivered into the box from out wide, but at a slightly differ angle and a flatter trajectory.

The common tactic is to line up a few of your taller players at the front post, the throw is delivered to their heads and they then flick the ball into the heart of the penalty area to be attacked by their colleagues.

Delivered correctly, the long throw can be just as effective as a corner or free kick.

Top Tips:

✓ Throw-In taker: As soon as you get the ball in your hands, immediately position it behind your head. If a teammate suddenly finds themselves in a bit of space you will be able to throw it to them straight away.

✓ When throwing the ball to your teammate, try to aim it to them so the ball is on its way down when they try to control it. It is much easier to control this way then if the ball has taken a bounce before it reaches your teammate.

Chapter 8

Fitness

Walk into any major soccer team training ground and you will see the players working on their fitness for as long, if not longer than they work on their skills. A player could have the most incredible skills you have ever seen, but if they don't have the fitness to compliment the skills, they are unlikely to be able to play to their true potential. If you want to become a great player, your fitness should be a huge part of your training regime! Fitness in soccer can be split into three broad sections; aerobic, strength, and speed & agility.

8.1 - Aerobic

It's obvious that soccer players must have high levels of aerobic fitness, but many people who don't play the game don't appreciate just how important aerobic fitness is.

How many times have you seen hugely important goals scored after the 85th minute? More often than not, this happens because one side is fitter than the other and can continue applying pressure until the final whistle.

But aerobic fitness isn't simply being able to run for a long time. Endurance is only one part of the aerobic attributes a player must possess. In a match, a player will be required to walk, jog, run, sprint, and run backwards while contesting in challenges, controlling the ball, jumping, and lunging. On average, a player will cover between 5.5 and 6.8 miles in a single match. That's a huge distance covered every time they take to the field. Of this distance:

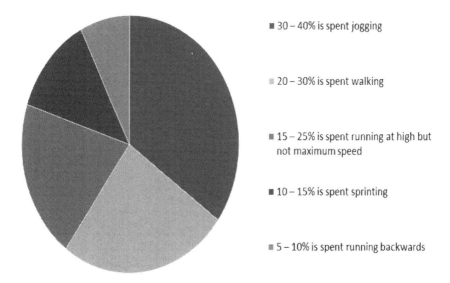

- 30 – 40% is spent jogging
- 20 – 30% is spent walking
- 15 – 25% is spent running at high but not maximum speed
- 10 – 15% is spent sprinting
- 5 – 10% is spent running backwards

These statistics demonstrate that players must possess a range of aerobic attributes to compete for 90 minutes. They must be able to sprint as often and as fast in the final 15 minutes of a match as they can in the first 15 minutes. They must also be able to rapidly switch from walking to sprinting or from jogging to running backwards.

Aerobic Training Techniques

- **Long Distance Running**

The simplest way to improve aerobic fitness is long distance running. Running at a comfortable pace for at least 40 minutes two times a week will strengthen respiration muscles and give you an extra edge towards the end of a match.

> *Top Tip:*
>
> ✓ If you find long distance running a tedious chore, here are a few things you could do to make it more engaging:
>
> - Find a running partner.
> - Time yourself and keep trying to beat your best time.
> - Change running locations.
> - Listen to music.
> - Create milestones and reward yourself for achieving them.

- **Intermittent Aerobic Course**

Creating a simple aerobic course using some cones can help to develop your aerobic, threshold, and sprinting capacity. Use five cones set up in a straight line, with each cone set 10 yards apart. Begin by slowly jogging one lap around the cones as a warm up.

1. To start the course, sprint from the first cone to the second cone, followed by jogging to the end cone.

2. Once you reach the end cone, run around it and sprint past two cones, followed by jogging back to the first cone.

3. This time, sprint from the first cone to the second last cone, followed by jogging to the end cone.

4. Once you reach the end cone, run around it and sprint back to the first cone.

Complete this circuit once and rest for one minute. Do one more set and rest for two minutes, followed by a third set.

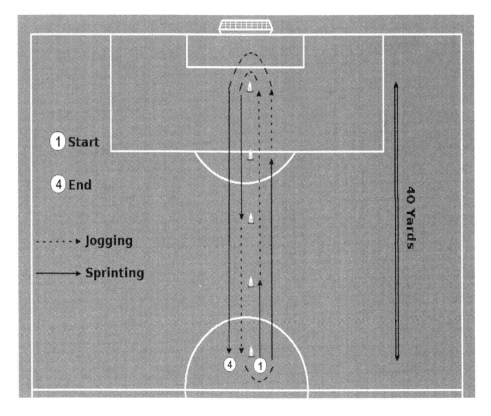

- **Fartlek Technique**

Notoriously hated by soccer players and athletes in general, but hugely beneficial, the Fartlek technique is a famous aerobic training method developed by Gösta Holmér in 1937. It is a form of long distance running where periods of fast running are combined with periods of slower running. There are numerous different types of Fartlek training sessions, but one that has been developed specifically for soccer is the Pyramid Fartlek Runs.

Prepare for the exercise by slowly jogging for a few minutes to get yourself warmed up. Begin by running for three minutes at a fast pace (just below sprinting). Then jog for 45 seconds and repeat twice. Once finished, rest for 4-5 minutes and repeat the set.

8.2 - Strength

Part of being the 'complete soccer player' is having upper body strength to hold off challenges, core body strength to maintain balance, and lower body strength to hit the ball with power. However, unlike athletes such as bodybuilders whose training is solely strength based, soccer players must combine strength with aerobic endurance, speed, and agility. Simply lifting weights may increase your size, bulk, and maximum strength, but it will also reduce your agility and endurance. There are two broad categories of strength which benefit soccer players:

i. **Muscular strength and power** is produced from both absolute strength and speed of movement. When a player increases their absolute power or their speed of movement, such as agility, they will increase their strength and muscular power. This allows them to be quicker off the mark in a foot race or to hit the ball with more explosive power.

ii. **Strength endurance** is how long you can maintain near full strength. It is pointless having the upper body strength to hold off an opponent if you can only maintain the power for a limited period of time.

When training in these categories, you can place focus on certain body parts to improve aspects of your game. Developing lower body strength is required for jumping, tackling, kicking the ball, and acceleration. Developing upper body strength is required for shielding the ball, blocking opponents, and overall power. Developing core strength is required for sudden twists, turns, starts, and stops.

Building your strength requires you to focus on areas which are specific to the position you play. Each position on a team requires different attributes, and concentrating on the specific strength training for your position will help you excel in your role on the team.

Goalkeepers require leg strength for jumping and powerful goal kicks, upper body strength for close contact situations against attacking players, and explosive speed to dive across the mouth of the goal when making a save. They must excel at quick and explosive movements which can be gained by developing lower body strength and core strength.

Defenders are traditionally known as the slowest players on the field due to their concentration on the development of strength and power over speed. Although, the best defenders in the world have found a way to maintain strength without reducing speed by working on a well-rounded strength training program which is usually maintained year-round.

Midfielders require the strength attributes of both a defender and a forward. They need to have powerful upper body strength to compete against opposing players and strong leg muscles when running, tackling and shooting.

Forwards require strong balance and agility which makes focusing on core strength the top priority. A great forward will have explosive speed to beat the defender or the offside trap and powerful leg muscles to strike the ball.

Strength Training Techniques

Core strength training

Building up core strength helps improve your balance, coordination, and stability on the field. Increasing core strength also links muscles to movements, making it the foundation for other types of strength training. Many core strength exercises are designed to train multiple joints and are performed using the whole body in a multidirectional movement. The following are some core strength exercises which can be performed at home using only a mat or carpeted floor. To gain the maximum effect from these exercises, repeat each in sets of five and build up to more sets as you improve.

Abdominal crunch: One of the most popular exercises used by athletes in virtually every sport, abdominal crunches can be extremely effective. Lie down on your back and place your feet on a wall so that your knees and hips are bent at a 90 degree angle. Tense your abdomen and raise your head and shoulders off the floor. Cross your arms on your chest to avoid straining your neck and hold the position for one second. Relax back into the start position and repeat.

Bridge: The bridge exercise is designed to improve the core strength of several muscles in one movement. Lie down on your back with your knees bent and your arms at your side. Make sure that your back is in a natural position and not pressed against the floor or arched. Tense your abdomen and raise your hips off the floor until they are aligned with your knees and shoulders. Hold the position for three deep inhalations, relax back into the start position, and repeat.

Single/Double leg abdominal press: The single and double leg abdominal press exercises offer flexibility and can affect numerous muscles responsible for core strength. The classic single leg abdominal press involves lying on your back with your knees bent and raising your right leg off the floor until you are in a position where your knee and hip are bent at a 90 degree angle. Press your right hand against your knee while using your abdominal muscles to pull your knee towards your hand. Hold the position for three deep inhalations, relax, and repeat. Variations of the exercise include using your opposite hand and opposite knee, placing your hand on the outside of your knee, and performing the exercise with both knees and hands at the same time (known as a double leg abdominal press).

Modified plank: The modified plank exercise is very effective in increasing core strength and can be performed in several variations. Begin by lying on your stomach and raising yourself so that you're resting on your knees and forearms, with your head and neck aligned with your back and shoulders directly above your elbows. Tighten your abdominal muscles and create tension by pressing your knees and elbows towards each other without them moving from their positions. Hold for 20-30 seconds, relax and repeat. Variations of the modified plank include resting on your toes instead of your knees and raising your right or left arm off the floor while creating tension or raising your left or right leg off the floor. The exercise can also be performed on your side to improve stability.

Superman: The superman exercise is designed to strengthen the core muscles in your lower back. Lie on your stomach and extend your arms out front, keeping your elbows slightly bent. Tighten your abdominal muscles and use your lower back muscles to lift your chest off the floor. Hold the position for one minute, rest for one minute and repeat. The exercise can also be performed using your legs, but due to risk of injury do not lift both your chest and legs at the same time.

Overall Strength, Power, and Strength Endurance Training

One of the best ways to build up overall strength, power, and strength endurance is by circuit training. Circuit training involves performing a group of exercises in a particular sequence and can be developed to target certain areas of the body. A circuit can consist of anything from 3 exercises to 10 or 12 exercises, but it is important to know your limit. Starting small and building up to more exercises is the best way to improve. The following are examples of circuit training which are designed to target specific areas of the body.

- **Lower Body Circuit Workout**

A lower body circuit workout concentrates on the leg muscles and consists of the following:

1. Dumbbell squat, raising to the calf (15 reps)
2. 30 second sprint on a stationary bike or a 100 meter sprint
3. Dumbbell side lunge (12 reps on each leg)
4. Physioball leg curl (15 reps)
5. 60 second sprint on a stationary bike

After completing the circuit, rest for one minute and repeat. Doing 3 or 4 sets of this circuit will greatly improve lower body strength, power, and strength endurance.

- **Upper Body Circuit Workout**

An upper body circuit workout concentrates on the abdomen and arm muscles, and consists of the following:

1. Dumbbell curl and press (12 reps)
2. Incline body row (12 reps)
3. Upper body step up (12 reps with each arm)
4. Cable pull-down to the front while seated (12 reps)
5. Push-ups on an incline (12 reps)

After completing the circuit, rest for one minute and repeat. Doing 3 or 4 sets of this circuit will greatly improve upper body strength, power, and strength endurance.

- **Total Body Circuit Workout**

A total body circuit workout would usually be used by players during the off-season to maintain their strength endurance. A total body circuit workout consists of the following:

1. Dumbbell hang (5 reps)
2. Dumbbell squat into an overhead press (5 reps)

3. Dumbbell forward lunge and curl (5 reps)

4. Dumbbell split (5 reps)

5. Dumbbell squat jump (5 reps)

After completing the circuit, rest for one minute and repeat. Doing 4 or 5 sets of this circuit will greatly improve total body strength, power, and strength endurance.

It is advisable to only do one of these workouts at a time, preferably giving yourself a day's rest before starting another workout.

8.3 - Speed & Agility

Having good speed and agility are attributes that almost every player needs. But these attributes are much more complex in soccer than simply being able to run quickly for a short period of time. For example, an athlete who runs the 100 meters sprint only requires some of the speed and agility attributes a soccer player must have.

During a typical match, a player will spend an average of 10-15% of the time sprinting which means they must also possess speed endurance, providing the means to run at top speed for a prolonged period of time. On top of speed endurance, they must have fast acceleration, be able to sprint with the ball, have the ability to quickly change direction, and perform agile movements.

Training and improving your speed and agility consists of several elements. First, there is absolute speed which is determined by your ability to run at top speed under varying conditions. A player who possesses a high level of absolute speed may have a yard of pace on their opponent which could be the difference between a scoring opportunity and a defensive clearance.

Second is acceleration which means how fast you can pick up speed. This can be very useful as it can give you a head start on your opponent in a foot race or help you dribble past an opponent.

Third is agility which relates to how quickly you can change direction without losing your balance or coordination. An agile player will have a high level of foot speed and be very nimble on the ball.

Fourth is speed endurance which relates to how long you can maintain near maximum speed. Although it is not a key attribute, it can certainly help if you play in a position that requires you to sprint up and down the field.

> **Top Tip:**
>
> ✓ As mentioned on chapter *1.4: Dribbling*, having a shorter stride length can improve your dribbling skills and ball control. The training techniques outlined below can be a great way to practice altering your stride length.

Speed & Agility Training Techniques

Plyometrics

Using plyometrics is one of the most effective ways to increase acceleration, explosive speed, and power. During plyometrics, muscles stretch rapidly before contraction, improving their strength and providing the ability to run faster and move with more agility. The following are some simple plyometric workouts for you to do:

- **Lateral Bounds**

  1. Balance on your right leg.

  2. Slightly bend your knee and sit into your hips, adding weight to the standing leg.

  3. Jump laterally as high and as far as you can, landing on your other leg.

  4. Absorb impact by landing in the same position as when you jumped.

  5. Swing your arms for extra power.

  6. Pause for 3 seconds and repeat.

  7. Complete 3-5 sets of 5-10 reps with a rest of two minutes between sets.

- **Explosive Push-Ups**

  1. Begin in the traditional push-up position.

  2. Slowly lower your chest to the floor and forcefully push yourself up so your hands don't touch the floor anymore.

  3. Land softly with elbows bent and repeat.

  4. Keep core muscles tightened throughout movement.

  5. Complete 4 sets of 5-10 reps with a rest of two minutes between sets.

- **Split-Jumps**

    1. Begin in a staggered stance with your right foot in front.

    2. Lower into a lunge, keeping your chest up and core muscles tight.

    3. Jump as high as you can, scissor-kick your legs, and land with your left leg forward.

    4. Alternate forward leg for each set.

    5. Complete 3-5 sets of 10-20 reps with a rest of 2 or 3 minutes between sets.

- **T-Hop Drill**

    1. Create a 'T' shape with tape on the ground, measuring roughly 2x2 feet.

    2. Begin by hopping with your feet together forwards and backwards along the vertical line of the 'T'.

    3. Progress to two-foot hops, diagonally, clockwise, and counter-clockwise laterally along the 'T'.

    4. Finish the set by hopping on one foot in all directions.

    5. The aim is to limit ground contact time as much as possible while moving as quickly as possible.

    6. Complete 20 seconds for each pattern for one set.

Speed, Speed Endurance, and Acceleration Drills

Speed drills are designed to stress your muscles to the maximum, so make sure you warm up properly and rest in between sessions. Muscles will regenerate the day after performing the actual exercise, so it is also important to limit speed drills to 2-3 times per week.

The best surface to use is a soft surface such as grass which lowers the risk of injury compared to a hard surface such as concrete. Warming up before performing a speed drill should take around 20 minutes and incorporate as many muscle groups as possible.

- **Acceleration**

To perform a speed drill focused on improving acceleration, place two cones around 20 yards apart. Begin at the first cone with your back facing towards the second cone. At a given signal, turn and sprint towards the second cone. As soon as you reach the second cone, turn on your heel and sprint back to the first cone. The key to this drill is in the acceleration after each turn.

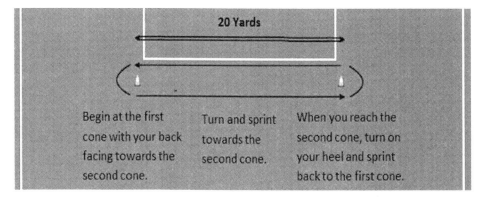

- **Maximum Speed and Endurance**

To improve your maximum speed, set up three cones in a straight line. The first two cones should be 30 yards apart, representing the actual distance you will be sprinting. The third cone should be at least 10 yards from the second cone.

Begin at the first cone and sprint to the second cone as fast as you can. Once you reach the second cone, decelerate until you reach the third cone and then jog slowly back to the first cone. The aim of the third cone in this drill is to discourage you from decelerating before you reach the second cone. To improve your speed endurance, increase the sprint distance to 75 yards.

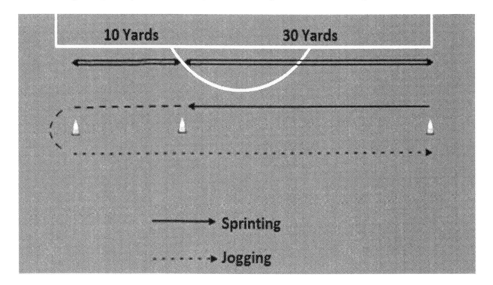

- **Speed Resistance**

This drill is designed to improve your ability to accelerate over the first few yards by developing your leg power. Set up two cones around 10-15 yards apart on an incline of around 30 degrees or on the beach. Ideally, you want to run where there is some kind of resistance. Begin at the first cone and sprint as fast as you can up the incline or along the beach until you reach the second cone. Make sure you take a longer recovery time in between sets as this drill is very intense.

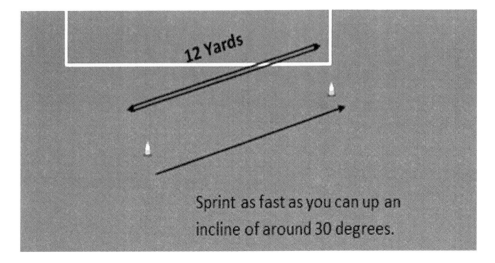

Agility and Acceleration Drills

Agility drills are designed to improve your balance, foot speed, body control, and coordination. Like speed drills, agility drills require a warm up of around 20 minutes, a rest between sets, and should only be performed 2-3 times per week.

Although agility drills aren't physically demanding, it is extremely easy to injure yourself while performing them if you haven't warmed up properly or if you push yourself too hard. Generally, agility drills are performed after the warmup and before the more exhausting drills.

- **Pro Agility**

To perform the pro agility drill, set up three straight lines situated 5 yards apart. Begin the drill on the middle line and sprint to the line on the right, touching it with your right hand. Quickly turn and sprint to the left line, touching it with your left hand. Finish the set by sprinting back to the middle line. This can be performed 3-5 times with a rest of around one minute between each set.

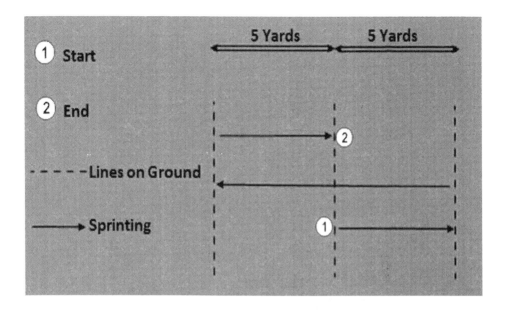

- **Slalom**

The slalom is a popular drill for wingers and can be performed with or without a ball. Set up 10 cones in a straight line, each 5 yards apart. Begin at the first cone and weave in and out of the course as quickly as possible. When you get to the end cone, jog slowly back to the first cone and repeat. To solely develop leg movement it is better to perform the drill without a ball.

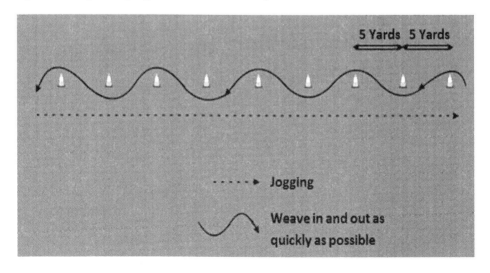

- **T-Drill**

The T-Drill is set up by arranging four cones in a 'T' shape with three cones forming the horizontal line on the 'T'. The three cones along the horizontal line of the 'T' should be 5 yards apart (cone C to the left, cone B in the middle, and cone D to the right) and the fourth cone at the bottom should be 10 yards from the middle cone (cone A).

Begin at cone 'A' and sprint to cone 'B', touching the cone then shuffling left to cone 'C'. Touch cone 'C' and shuffle right to cone 'D'. Touch cone 'D' and shuffle left to cone 'B', backpedalling to cone 'A' to complete the drill.

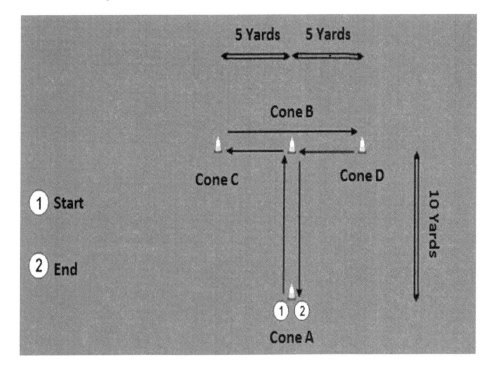

8.4 - Testing Your Fitness

As a player or a coach, you may want to test your fitness or the fitness of your squad to see which areas require improvement. You may also want to test your fitness if you are not yet 100% sure which position suits you best.

Gathering the results from fitness tests can help you discover which attributes you possess and which position they are most suited to. There are numerous fitness tests which have been devised, with the best listed below.

- **VO2 Max**

The VO2 max test can be used to test the aerobic fitness of a player. The test relies on contributions from the lungs, heart, blood, and active muscles which when combined provide a measurement in how aerobically fit a player is. The typical score in a VO2 max test for a professional aged between 22 and 28 (male and female) is 50-64 and for a regular person of the same age is 33-52. There are a number of physical evaluations which determine a VO2 max score in both direct and indirect methods. A popular direct method is known as the 'Bruce protocol', however, it involves the use of various exercise equipment which isn't readily available to everyone. Indirect methods are more widely used by coaches and individuals and require little or no exercise equipment.

A popular indirect way to test your VO2 max is the 'Balke 15 Minute Run'. For this test you will require a stop watch and a standard 400 meter running track. Once you have warmed up, run continuously around the running track for 15 minutes exactly. The aim is to maintain a steady pace throughout the run, without sprinting towards the end or walking halfway through. The distance you cover can then be converted into a predicted VO2 max using the following guide:

Distance (in meters)	Predicted VO2 max (ml/kg/min)
5200	70.0
4800	65.5
4400	61.0
4000	56.5
3600	51.5
3200	47.0
2800	42.5
2400	38.0

As you can see, a professional aged between 22 and 28 should be able to run between 3,600 and 4,800 meters during this test. It is worth noting that your score isn't a direct prediction of performance. When using the training methods described in the aerobic section, your VO2 max score will naturally increase.

- **Yo-Yo Intermittent Test**

The Yo-Yo Intermittent test is another way of testing your aerobic fitness. This test is regularly used in professional soccer to evaluate an individual's ability to repeatedly perform intervals over a prolonged period of time. This kind of fitness is essential in a match, where you will need to be able to perform to your maximum ability in intervals. The test uses the BeepTest software (many of you will be familiar with it from the beep test in high school), marking cones, and a measuring tape. The test also has a beginner's level 1 and an advanced level 2, depending on how fit you are when taking the test. To perform the test:

1. Place two cones 5 meters apart and a third cone 20 meters away to create a straight line.

2. Begin on the cone in the middle and start running towards the cone which is 20 meters away when the first beep on the BeepTest software sounds.

3. When the next beep sounds, run back towards the middle cone.

4. A recovery time of 10 seconds is provided between each run out and back where you must walk or jog around the first cone (5 meters away).

5. If you do not complete a successful round trip in the allocated time a warning is received.

6. If you do not complete a successful round trip for a second time, the test is finished.

For more advanced levels, half the recovery distance and time.

The score is calculated by recording the total distance covered before becoming unable to complete a round trip for a second time. A formula is then used to calculate the test results:

Yo-Yo IR test: VO2max = distance covered (in meters) x 0.0084 + 36.4

The average result for a professional is between 54 and 64. As the Yo-Yo Intermittent test was designed specifically for soccer players, it is an excellent way to evaluate your aerobic fitness. The stricter you run the test, the more accurate your results.

- **One Repetition Maximum**

The One Repetition Maximum Bench Press Test (1-RM Test) is a popular method of measuring muscle strength. The test measures the absolute or maximal weight a person can lift with one repetition. The idea of the test is to reach the maximum weight before fatiguing the muscles.

Once you have warmed up, select a weight which is achievable. DO NOT select a weight which is too heavy as you can suffer severe damage. If you are able to lift the weight selected, take a rest for several minutes and increase the weight. Continue until you can only repeat one full and correct weight lift of a weight.

Once you have found the maximum weight you can lift in one repetition, record the details of the weight. It is also worth recording other attempts leading to the maximum weight as this can help you in subsequent tests.

It is possible that three or five repetitions are used when doing the 1-RM test. This is particularly true for beginners who may be able to lift less weight for a greater number of reps. If this is the case, you can enter the weight used and the number of reps you could perform before having to stop. This will still provide an accurate 1-RM score.

To calculate your score use the following formula:

1-RM = weight lifted x (1 + (reps/30))

- **30m Sprint Test**

The 30m Sprint test is designed to test both speed and power. It can be used to evaluate your ability to build up acceleration from a standing start to maximum speed. To perform the test, you will need cones, a stopwatch, and someone to time you.

Mark out a straight line of 30 meters with a cone at both ends, and warm up for around 10 minutes. After the warm up, sprint as fast as possible over the 30 meter track. The person timing the run with a stopwatch should begin timing when your foot first touches the floor and stop the watch once your torso has fully crossed the second cone. Conduct the test three times and use the best score to assess your performance.

This test is extremely relevant in soccer as many sprint races to gain possession of the ball take place over this sort of distance. Improving your result in the 30m Sprint Test can be achieved by using the techniques outlined in the strength and speed sections.

- **Illinois Test**

The Illinois test is commonly used in numerous sports as a way of measuring a person's ability to quickly change position and direction. The course for an Illinois test is 10 meters in length and 5 meters in width. Eight cones are required; one to mark the start, one to mark the finish, two to mark turning points and four in the center of the course. The four cones in the center of the course should be of equal distance (3.3 meters) apart. The start cone, finish cone, and two turning point cones should form a square enclosing the center cones.

To perform the test, begin at the start cone lying on your front with your head at the starting line and hands by your shoulders. When the stopwatch is started, get up as quickly as possible and run in a straight line to the first turning cone. Run around the cone and back to the other end of the course towards the first middle cone. Weave in between the four middle cones, circling the end cone and weaving back to the first middle cone. From there, run to the second turning cone and down to the finish cone. If any cones are knocked over, the test must be performed again.

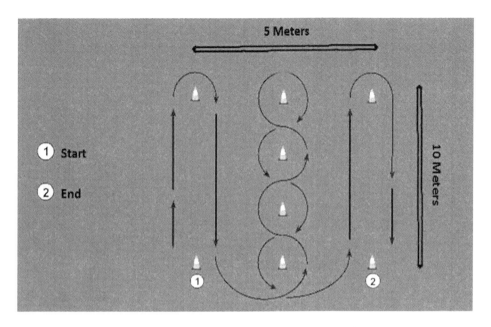

Calculate your time to two decimal points and use the chart below to see how you did. (Based on ages 16 -19)

Rating	**Males** *Time (in seconds)*	**Females** *Time (in seconds)*
Excellent	<15.2	<17.0
Above Average	15.2 - 16.1	17.0 - 17.9
Average	16.2 - 18.1	18.0 - 21.7
Below Average	18.2 - 19.3	21.8 - 23.0
Poor	>19.3	>23.0

Using this test is a great way to test your acceleration, speed, and agility. The movements required to complete this test are very relevant to the movements you will make during a match. To improve on your results, use the training techniques outlined in the speed and agility section.

Chapter 9

Health & Nutrition

Maintaining a healthy body is crucial if you plan to maximise your ability. The beautiful game is, by its very nature, a physically demanding sport, and only those with a great level of fitness and general health are likely to prosper.

Getting fit and adopting a balanced diet and healthy lifestyle can have several benefits:

- ✓ Improved strength, speed and fitness.

- ✓ Minimised risk of injury.

- ✓ The ability to maintain and maximize your performance for 90 minutes.

- ✓ Recovery time between games/after a training session is minimised.

The truth is that you don't have to be an absolute angel when it comes to your diet to be a good player – even elite athletes enjoy the odd piece of cake, the odd alcoholic beverage and even the occasional Big Mac and Fries every once in a while! But knowing what to eat, and when to eat it, will help you to enhance the effectiveness of your training and achieve an extra percentage in your match performance....and that can be the all-important difference between success and failure.

9.1 - Preventing Injuries

Soccer, at all levels, is a high impact sport, and one that requires the individual to use an incredible number of their muscle groups – including some that you simply would not use in any other sporting or everyday situation.

As a consequence, injuries are commonplace and often unavoidable - even the fittest and most in-shape player will suffer from the odd muscle tweak or knock. Collisions take place all over the field, these are inevitable, and mistimed tackles can often result in painful cuts, bruises and swelling, whilst explosive bursts of speed can strain or in the worst cases tear a muscle.

Injuries can also be caused by using the wrong equipment, e.g. wearing the wrong type of shoes on wet/soft/hard ground, and many aches and pains can also be the result of pushing yourself too hard in the gym or out on the training field.

Fortunately, you can often prevent - or at least minimise - some of the more niggling injuries that can blight a player's season by taking some proactive and preventative steps. Some are obvious, some less so, but all should be undertaken to keep your body in peak condition:

Warming Up and Stretching

Warming up and stretching the key muscle groups is an absolutely vital process; not only in preventing injury but also in maximising your performance. Many players want to get out onto the field and practise their passing or shooting as soon as they can, but without a proper warm-up routine, the chances that they will suffer muscle or joint damage is greatly increased.

Furthermore, stretching the muscles correctly will also enable you to achieve the full range of movement, which is far more preferable than expecting muscles that are tense and 'cold' to give you a burst of pace or a quick change in direction. It's worth noting that improving your muscle flexibility will ultimately help to increase your speed and agility....and this could make all the difference to your game.

But, realistically, the key to an effective warm-up programme is to prevent injuries before they can occur; because prevention is better than cure.

The Keys to a Good Warm-Up

The basic premise behind a warm-up is to prepare the body for the more dynamic exercises and strenuous activities that are set to come its way. A game of soccer - even a casual kick-about between friends - places incredible strain on muscles and joints, so it is best to prepare these for dynamic activity. If you don't, a nasty injury is an accident just waiting to happen.

And so a good warm-up needs to:

- Increase body and muscle temperature.

- Increase heart rate.

- Practice a wide range of movements relevant to the sport.

- Enable you to be in peak condition for when the match starts.

A good warm-up routine is like a car going up through the gears, with the aim of preparing the key muscle groups for dynamic activity. Like any motor vehicle, if your body goes from first gear to fifth then you are likely to experience serious problems, which is why a smooth progression is far more effective. So keep it nice and steady when you first switch your engine on and slowly increase the tempo once you're warm and your core is activated.

Start with the gentlest and most 'passive' stretches and exercises first, before slowly progressing through the gears to more dynamic movements. A good warm-up programme will look something similar to the following:

1. Initial Gentle Warm-Up

This is a crucial stage of the warm-up and MUST NOT be skipped or overlooked as you prepare your body for action. It is this stage which is the most important in transforming your muscles from their relaxed or inactive state to readiness for physical exertion.

Failure to complete this part of the process, and skipping to Steps 2 or 3 in this guide, will potentially result in you suffering an injury or aggravating an underlying problem before you have even taken to the field of play.

So you need to be aiming for a light period of physical activity here. It could even be running a lap of the field; starting at a slow jog before slowly increasing to a slightly faster pace. This will help to prepare your key muscle groups for the static stretches to be carried out in Step 2. The aim of this gentle warm-up is to increase the blood flow to the muscles and their internal temperature, which will result in safer and more effective stretching.

As a result, a successful initial gentle warm-up should leave you feeling a bit out of breath, perspiring ever so slightly and your body temperature heightened.

2. Static Stretching

There are two general forms of stretching: static and dynamic. Static is the safest and less strenuous type, as these are performed from a stationary position, and so this should be your first port of call once you've completed your initial warm-up.

Static stretching offers a minimal threat of injury if executed correctly, and is the perfect platform to prepare your body for the rigours of exercise. Even so, you need to still stretch 'within yourself' and not push your body too hard at this stage.

A static stretch is one that places a muscle under a moderate amount of tension from a standing position. You will feel the muscle contract slightly, and holding this position for 5-10 seconds will help to stretch, lengthen and release the muscle fibres; which results in a greater range of muscle movement and flexibility. This aids your agility and enables you to perform changes in direction and bursts of speed with far greater ease.

Remember, DO NOT stretch too far or too hard at this point, and do not get into positions which are uncomfortable for you to hold as this will be counter-productive to your warm-up regime.

You will shortly move onto a range of stretches and exercises that are designed specifically for soccer, but at this stage you need to be static stretching your core muscle groups as well as the glutes, hamstrings, thighs and calves, in order to move onto Step 3 with confidence.

- Toe Touch – from a standing position slowly bring your arms towards your toes. You should feel your calves and hamstrings stretching nicely.

- Groin Stretch – Take a wide stance with your feet turned out approximately 45 degrees. Bend your right knee and gradually shift your weight to your right leg, keeping your left leg straight. Place both your hands on your right knee for support. Repeat on other side. You can increase the starting distance between your feet for a greater stretch.

- Quad Stretch – stand on one leg and raise the other behind you, gently grabbing the ankle and bringing it in slowly to your buttocks. Repeat with other leg.

- Hamstring Stretch – Sitting down, stretch your legs out in front of you while keeping your back upright. Bend your left leg keeping your left foot flat on the floor. Slowly reach forward and try to touch your right toe with both hands. Bend from your waist keeping your lower back flat and your head up. Repeat for the other leg.

3. Soccer Specific Dynamic Stretching

Once you've achieved a good foundation to your warm-up by stretching and lengthening the key muscle groups, you can now prepare with some dynamic stretches using specific movements and stretches that are vital to a soccer player.

These should only be undertaken when your body feels completely loose and supple after undertaking the first two steps of this guide. If you have yet to do that or feel any slight twinge or niggle in a muscle or joint, then YOU SHOULD NOT carry out this stage for fear of worsening the problem. Start again from Step 1 and work your way through to Step 3.

The difference between a static stretch and a dynamic one is that the dynamic tends to combine the stretching maneuver with a controlled, secondary movement; such as a bounce or swinging motion. The aim of this is to take the muscles beyond their usual range of movement, and thus prepare them for the often extreme requirements of competitive sport.

Now more vigorous stretches can be employed as you prepare for kick off or the start of a training session. Consider this a 'rehearsal' for the match itself, and so stretches and exercises that replicate match day scenarios are advised. These include sprint shuttle runs, burpees and star jumps, all of which are highly effective in imitating the movements undertaken in the average game of soccer.

A few dynamic soccer-specific exercises to consider include:

- High Knees – Gently jog and bring your knees up so that your thighs run parallel to the ground. Some people put their hands out at waist height and touch them with their thighs on the way up.

- Lunge Walk – As you walk, extend your legs in a lunge movement and then continue moving forwards once more and repeat with the opposite leg. A great exercise that stretches everything from hips to toes.

- Sideways/Backwards Run – A sideways and backwards run stretches out the hip flexor muscles, the groins and the inner thighs in a more dynamic way to forward running. Use the width of the field and do a circuit of each simultaneously.

These dynamic movements should be soccer-specific, and most crucially they should remain controlled at all times – a rash dynamic movement can result in rather unwanted injuries, strains and muscle tears.

Once this part of the warm-up regime has been completed, you will be ready to take to the field in prime physical condition.

Warming Up and Stretching: A Summary

Whether you are preparing for a big match or a training session, warming up properly and stretching safely are absolutely imperative. This will help to keep you healthy, injury-free and also allows you to physically be at the peak of your powers.

Sometimes carrying out an intense 20 minute warm-up regime is impossible due to time limitations, so as an absolute minimum Steps 1 and 2 of the above guide need to be undertaken. You will be thankful for this advice when you remain fit and healthy whilst your teammates are struck down by aches, pains and injuries!

An adequate warm-up will also give you the confidence in your body to succeed, in that you will know you are operating at your physical peak. How often have you seen a player pressed into action for their team despite carrying an injury, and their subsequent performance then being way below par.

As you will find out elsewhere in this book, being confident and in control of the psychological aspects of your game are absolutely critical. But looking after your body gives you the best chance to succeed.

Top Tips:

✓ The quad, groin and hamstring muscles are the most susceptible to injury and therefore require the most attention when stretching.

✓ When you start your stretches, begin with short, gentle stretches, increasing the length and intensity gradually.

✓ Only stretch to the point of mild discomfort. If you feel pain, stop.

✓ Don't bounce or overstretch while static stretching. This can cause muscle strains and major injuries.

The Right Equipment

Of course, utilising the right equipment will also help you to avoid unnecessary injury. The first port of call for players at all levels is to purchase a sturdy pair of shin guards. These are increasingly comfortable thanks to modern innovations (gone are the days when players would push screwed-up balls of newspaper down their socks for protection!), and their role is two-fold:

- To prevent bruising, swelling and bone damage from collisions and impact.
- To prevent cuts and lacerations from dangerous tackles.

All of the above are painful injuries that can see you sidelined from the game for days and sometimes even weeks, so investing in a decent pair of shin guards is compulsory.

Suited and Booted

Thanks to the latest technologies and an ever-changing marketplace, soccer shoe design has undergone incredible improvements over the years. Boots are now manufactured from more durable yet lightweight materials, which enable you to sprint, jump, twist and turn with less pressure applied to your feet, ankles and knees when compared to the heavyweight leather shoes of yesteryear.

There are also a number of different cleat options, which are suited for varying types of surface. The old-fashioned cleated boots are still highly popular as they offer plenty of traction and support on typically soft and boggy ground, whilst newer innovations such as blades are worn by those who play more regularly on hard ground. It really is up to you which shoe you feel more comfortable with; and this should be your ultimate guide, not the brand name or street cred that certain shoes afford you!

However, it is often impractical and financially prohibitive for the amateur player to own more than one pair of shoes, so make sure you use the following information when purchasing your next pair:

- Traditional Cleats – for soft ground, traditionally worn in the UK in the harsh winter months.

- Blades – used on hard ground or harder surfaces that have been moistened slightly by a rain shower.

- Moulded – used on harder surfaces too and likely to be worn in the UK at the start and end of the season where the ground is a lot firmer.

- Astroturf – these are worn on rock hard ground that simply will not accept a cleat of any kind. Perfect for summer leagues and artificial grass surfaces.

Finders Keepers

These days goalkeepers aren't left in the shade either. Keepers throughout the years have always worn a padded shirt, particularly around the elbows, to help minimise the damage caused to the arms and elbows from diving to stop the ball, and now there are even different types of gloves to suit different needs.

Numerous options are available in terms of cut, padding and cushioning, and really the best advice that any aspiring goalkeeper can be given is to head to their nearest sports shop, try on a few different pairs and go for the pair which simply feels the best.

9.2 - Looking After your Body

The fitter you are, the less likely you are to pick up an injury: it really is as simple as that. Most muscle injuries occur when you are tired and fatigued, as your respiratory system is made to work harder and thus blood flow is concentrated away from the key soccer muscle groups.

Being fit on a level relevant to your output during the 90 minutes is essential. Of course, fitness levels are generally different for each player on the field: a central midfielder needs to get up and down and is therefore likely to be fitter than, say, a central defender, for example.

You should know yourself whether you are already fit enough to meet the demands of your position and the intensity that you play, or if more work on your stamina needs to be done. If you can't play 90 minutes without a significant loss of energy, then you are at risk of serious injury as your muscles become fatigued. Cramp is the least of your worries!

Cool Down and Recovery

One severely overlooked phase of the injury prevention process is cooling down correctly after a period of activity. This will help to reduce the amount of muscle ache experienced once the exercise is finished, and more importantly minimise the damage caused by minor underlying injuries in the short term.

The benefits of adequate cooling down on long-term injury prevention are clear too. Research has proven that stretching muscles properly after playing sport, and graduating their progress from active to inactive slowly rather than immediately, will significantly reduce your chances of suffering from a recurring injury.

Cooling down properly will help you to slow your heart rate down and improve your flexibility, and so its importance to your welfare and sporting prowess should not be underestimated.

The average cool down can take just five minutes, and consists of:

- A gentle jog at a slowly decelerating pace

- Glute stretches

- Hamstring stretches

- Thigh stretches

- Calf stretches

Remember, you're not warming these muscles up but cooling down, so the intensity of your stretches needs to be far more generous. It's simply a way of bringing your internal temperature down after the rollercoaster of motions that a soccer match offers, and allowing your muscles to relax. A good analogy is when you cook a steak in a hot pan and then allow it to rest on the side for a while before eating.

In a rather more extreme example, many professional sportsmen and women now jump into an ice bath straight after a match. Talk about bringing your body temperature down! This will also help to treat any niggles, bumps or bruises before they have a chance to manifest themselves further. But it's certainly not for the faint hearted, so don't consider it a required part of your cool down plan.

Allow Your Body to Fully Recover After an Injury

Despite all of the best preparation and intentions, sometimes injuries are simply unavoidable: sport, and soccer in particular, is just too unpredictable to know what's around the corner. Look at the number of injuries that the elite players pick up, despite being in the best possible shape. Unfortunately, injuries for athletes are just a fact of life.

There are, generally, two types of injury: acute pains that are very targeted and which the individual knows exactly when and where they occur. For example, an ankle strain will be very acute and painful, with tenderness and restricted movement noticeable straight away. This will likely have been caused by a quick change of direction where part of the body's weight is heading in a different direction completely.

And then there are the slow-burning injuries that you may not notice for hours after the event. One such example is minor knee ligament damage, with the release of pain and bruising tending to take a few hours after the trauma has occurred.

It is important to identify the injury as soon as possible too, as this will enable you to treat it and move forward with a recovery and rehabilitation plan. It may be obvious what your injury is, and thus you can treat yourself at home. In other cases, where the pain is acute or the injury worsens within a few days, you may want to visit your local doctor's surgery for a more informed opinion and diagnosis.

Home Treatment

Often it is easy to treat minor injuries at home using everyday products and a simple rehabilitation programme which slowly increases in intensity from complete rest to gentle exercise.

A sensible approach would include:

- ✓ Resting the affected muscle or body part for 48-72 hours at least – and longer where pain persists.

- ✓ Applying an ice pack during this time if appropriate (e.g. the area is not cut/lacerated). You can make an ice pack at home by wrapping ice cubes in a towel or old t-shirt and applying it to the area for a couple of minutes.

- ✓ Take over-the-counter pain medication picked up from your local store to help combat the pain.

- ✓ If it is a muscle injury, slowly start to introduce static stretches into your daily routine. These should start gentle and slowly increase in intensity (e.g. holding the stretch for 10 seconds). This will help to strengthen the muscle after any loss or wastage suffered during the repair process.

Remember, if the pain persists and your symptoms don't seem to improve within a few days or weeks, your doctor should be your first port of call. If they cannot help you, they may refer you to a specialist service such as a physiotherapist, for further treatment and support.

Common Injuries

Whilst injuries are unpredictable by their very nature, there is a common set of ailments that affect players of all abilities and positions. These are, unsurprisingly, situated in the leg joints mostly, as they are the muscle groups which tend to bear the brunt of our movements and dynamic shifts in weight.

Being able to identify your injury and the steps required to help it get better are important both in the short and long-term. No player wants to miss games through ongoing injuries – especially those which could heal quicker with an effective rehabilitation programme.

• Hamstring Tear/Strain

The hamstrings remain the most commonly damaged muscles in soccer, with a tear or strain usually caused by sudden shifts in direction or speed. Hamstring injuries are also particularly common amongst amateur athletes who don't warm up and stretch properly (you have been warned!).

A hamstring injury can be a strange one to experience: the individual may feel a 'popping' sensation at the back of their leg, and this can occur anywhere from just above the back of the knee to as high as the buttocks.

The pain is severe and immediate, and the only course of action is to rest up for a few weeks and wait for the damage to repair itself. Once it has, a gentle programme of static stretches can be introduced to strengthen and lengthen the muscle, with dynamic exercise to follow at least a fortnight later.

• Ankle Sprains

Another hugely common injury suffered by soccer players is ankle strains. As you can imagine, when you twist and turn at great speed or intensity you are essentially putting your whole body weight through your ankle joint, and this can have a huge stress and impact on the area.

Changing direction, an awkward fall or an impact collision can all cause an ankle strain, which occurs when one or more of the ligaments stretches to beyond its natural range of movement.

There are two types of ankle strain: an inversion sprain occurs when the ankle is 'rolled over' inwardly, e.g. the foot faces inwards. An eversion sprain is when the ankle is rolled outwards.

An ankle strain can be incredibly painful, with an intense ache felt around the ankle joint, swelling, bruising and tenderness, and an inability to put any weight on your foot. Further aggravation will be experienced if the strain is a) not treated correctly, and b) an effective rehabilitation programme is not implemented and stuck to.

With an ankle strain, rest is the only medicine. Apply ice at regular intervals to help with the pain and swelling, and be prepared to sit out from soccer for a few weeks.

- The Dreaded Cruciate Ligament Injury

With the sheer amount of intense pressure and velocity that is placed through the knee joints during a match, it is no surprise that knee injuries are so commonplace. The worst of these, the torn ACL (Anterior Cruciate Ligament), can end careers and have a permanent impact on the way the sufferer leads their life.

The ACL attaches the Tibia (which is your shin bone) to your Femur (the thigh bone). As such, you can probably imagine the important role it plays not only in supporting your movements in sport but also in everyday life.

Most ACL injuries come as a player twists in the opposite direction to their predominant motion, and this pressure becomes too much for the joint to take. A tear is the most severe outcome, with the pain immediate and debilitating.

It is highly unlikely that your ACL tear won't be detected by a paramedic or medical professional straight away – the pain will be so severe that you will need immediate medical assistance; you certainly won't be able to put any weight on the leg.

Minor ACL strains are possible too, and this will cause instability, pain and inflammation in the knee. You won't be able to straighten your leg, and the swelling will be rather spectacular. As such, rest and ice are needed in the immediate aftermath of an ACL strain, and then a slow rehabilitation process to strengthen the area should follow.

Nobody likes to suffer an injury of any kind, but an ACL tear is certainly one to avoid at all costs.

- Concussion

A concussion can often follow a blow to the head, and this is particularly the case when two players clash heads when challenging for an aerial ball. It is very important that any head injury, however seemingly minor, is treated with caution, as the knock-on effects of poor treatment and mis-diagnosis can be disastrous.

A concussion is a minor traumatic brain injury, and as such should be treated with the utmost respect. Common signs of a concussion include one or more of:

- Loss of consciousness

- Short term memory loss

- Double vision or 'seeing stars'

- Confusion and delayed reactions

The key with a head injury is to understand when it is appropriate to seek professional medical help. If any of the above symptoms persist, rather than being just temporary side effects, then a trip to the hospital is needed. Persistent headaches are also a cause for concern, as is drowsiness, loss of balance, difficulties concentrating and noticeable mood swings. Any of these could be a sign of something more serious as a result of your knock to the head.

If you suffer a head injury of any kind during training or a match, it is imperative that you leave the field of play immediately and seek further help as soon as possible if symptoms persist. A second opinion can never hurt, and it really is better to be safe than sorry as far as head injuries are concerned.

9.3 - Your Diet and You

Food is fuel for the body, and as such you can only get out what you put in. If you gorge on takeaway meals and fried food regularly, then you are unlikely ever to meet your sporting potential. On the other hand, if you enjoy a healthy, balanced diet then you are giving yourself the best chance of getting into optimum shape and achieving your very best.

Think of it like a car. If you put in the wrong kind of fuel, then the car simply won't work. If you put in the right fuel, it will be a smooth and reliable ride.

A poor diet can contribute to tiredness and sluggishness during and after physical activity, which will affect both your performance out on the field and your recovery afterwards. Your stamina and speed will be limited, you will not be able to train as hard, and you won't be able to keep up with the pace of play.

This book is all about helping you to maximise your performance and achieve your absolute potential on the soccer field. But many of the basic tenets of this happen away from the field and begin at home. Eating the right foods at the right times is paramount to this.

A Healthy Diet – the Essential Building Blocks

There are some food groups that are necessary components of a balanced diet, and these should be considered the foundations to the house (body) you want to build.

The key is balance, so a selection of each consumed on a rotational basis (with carbohydrates specifically on 'active' days such as training or matches) is the best way to go:

- Simple Carbohydrates (sweets, cakes, soft drinks, etc)

- Complex Carbohydrates (white bread, rice, pasta, etc)

- Protein (Chicken, eggs, milk, etc)

- Vitamins and Minerals (fruit, vegetables, seeds, etc)

- Fibre (some cereals, beans, peas, etc)

- Saturated (butter, cheese, cream) and Unsaturated Fats (oily fish, nuts, sunflower oil)

The truth is that a healthy, balanced diet comprises various amounts of each of these food groups. Naturally, you want to intake more 'goodness' than 'bad', and so vitamins and minerals should feature more heavily in your diet than fatty, carb-heavy meals.

But carbs have their place, particularly when leading an active lifestyle. They are interesting as they are vital in heightening glycogen levels – which is responsible for energy production, and so intaking carbohydrates prior to a match or training session is advisable, rather than frowned upon. Players with low glycogen levels tend to 'run out of steam' later in games if their natural fitness isn't exceptionally high, and therefore most of us need a 'carb store' to help see us through to the bitter end.

A word of caution though: complex carbohydrates turn into fat when they are not 'exercised', so if you are undergoing a period of rest or inactivity then do try to steer clear of carbs and instead seek an alternative such as pulses and beans.

Clever Carbs

Many soccer players and athletes are misguided in their attempts to create a carb store. Many will sit down with a huge plate of pasta or a bowl of rice before they embark on a period of activity, but this is the worst idea imaginable as it can often leave us feeling heavy and unable to perform at the peak of our physical powers. This is because of the fat and gluten content that these contain.

Instead, slowly introduce carbs throughout the day through clever snacking. Some great sources of carbohydrates that are low in fat include:

- ✓ Fruit: Bananas, strawberries, peaches, apricots

- ✓ Muesli Bars

- ✓ Yoghurts

- ✓ Rice Pudding

- ✓ Bagels

As you will notice, all of these products are commonly consumed for breakfast: with the notion that they slowly release energy throughout the day. If you can get into a routine of eating one or more of these sources on training or match day and lowering your intake of fatty carbs, then you are sure to notice the difference in your energy levels out on the field.

What to Eat Before and After a Match

Eating well before a game is necessary in maximising your performance, and also tucking into good food after a match will also aid your recovery. There's no harm in a celebratory meal if you have just won a big match of course, but everything in moderation is key.

- Pre-Match

The ideal make-up of your pre-match meal is:

Carbohydrate (medium portion) + vegetables (medium) + protein (small)

In combination, proteins and carbohydrates can cause problems with digestion, which is why only a small portion of protein, perhaps grilled fish or chicken breast, is recommended.

The carbohydrate will help to create glucose in the blood for energy, with research suggesting that eating 2-3 hours before kick-off is the optimum time for a soccer player. It's not too long that the added energy is burned off (and don't forget we are very active when we are nervous), but not too short a timeframe that the glycogen hasn't filtered into your blood flow.

- Post-Match

Once you have completed your warm down and have showered and changed, try to find the time to eat around 30 minutes to one hour after the final whistle. This is because your body's unique window of recovery requires you to feed it fuel to help repair and re-grow any muscle tissue and cells damaged during the course of the match. To achieve this, the glycogen levels in your body need to be increased through carbohydrate and (minimal) protein intake.

So at this precise moment, pasta, rice with fish, turkey or eggs are the best things to eat. In this way, you can maximise your body's recovery and reduce your suffering from fatigue during your next training session or match.

Hydration is Key

It's not just eating right that is crucial to a player's daily cycle: keeping hydrated before, during and after activity is equally as important. Water plays a dual role in keeping you healthy, as it regulates your body temperature and keeps you cool while transporting nutrients through the blood to give you energy.

It's no coincidence that people who are suffering from dehydration experience fatigue, muscle cramping and dizziness. Although this is an extreme example, keeping yourself well hydrated will clearly have enormous benefits to your performance out on the field, especially when the weather is hot and there is little cloud cover.

Every individual is different, and so there are no exact rules in terms of the amount of water you should be drinking. But obviously you need to consider your size, fitness levels and the temperature you are active in, as these will all have an impact on your hydration.

The American Council on Exercise has conducted extensive research into this very subject, and they suggest the following regime:

- 17-20 ounces of water (approx. 0.5 litres) around three hours prior to exercise.

- 8 ounces prior to kick off (approx. 0.2 litres).

- If possible, 7-10 ounces every 15 minutes during the match/training.

- 8 ounces immediately following the match/training session.

This is only a guide of course, but is a good way of regimenting your water intake and maintaining your hydration levels.

In most cases, water is all you need to stay adequately hydrated. But for those of who want to enhance your performances even further, specialised energy drinks can help to provide additional electrolytes and nutrients to keep you energised for even longer.

As with water, taking on small amounts of energy drinks at regular intervals – rather than downing a whole bottle – is important to ensure glycogen levels remain at a nice constant and thus the risk of bloating or stomach cramps is avoided.

Do always take the time to read the labels of each brand of sports drink carefully too. Some contain massive quantities of calories & sugar, some salt, and some caffeine, so getting a healthier balance of the three is naturally the preferred option.

Types of Foods to Avoid

Whilst sometimes it is fine to treat ourselves to those tasty meals and snacks - a slice of pizza here and a piece of chocolate cake there won't completely ruin your efforts to get fit and in great shape - making a habit of it is not advisable.

Maintaining a balanced diet that aids the body's nutritional performance is fundamental to enhancing your game out on the field, and as such there are a number of foods or food groups that need avoiding like the plague.

- Sugary Foods

Whilst nibbling on sweets or drinking a high sugar content drink is thought to give an energy boost; research has found that in fact the exact opposite is true. Instead, the empty calories result in what is known as Rebound Hypoglycaemia, which you may otherwise know as a 'sugar crash'. In a match, this could happen midway through the half and leave you on jelly legs – leaving your teammates high and dry.

- Fried Food

It is very important that you avoid fried foods, particularly on a match day or just before a training session. This is because they take longer to break down in the stomach, and this act in itself uses energy. So rather than adding anything of nutritional value, fried food actually negates the hard work you have done.

- Coffee

Similarly to the sweets argument above, there is a commonly-held misconception that drinking coffee can somehow increase energy and focus. Again, this is a short-term gain for a long-term loss. For 5-10 minutes you may notice an increase in concentration levels and a 'buzz' that the caffeine creates, but this adrenal stimulation is always followed by a bad case of fatigue and that old elephant in the room, Rebound Hypoglycaemia.

- Fizzy Drinks

The standard 330ml can of your favourite fizzy drink contains approximately 10 teaspoons of sugar. You probably don't even need me to tell you how bad this is for you, but as you found out above sugar is a source of 'bad energy' – a short-term gain for a long-term loss.

Carbonated drinks lead to increased calorie intake and, in some cases, calcium depletion, and whilst you may experience a brief upturn in energy, before long you will notice that fatigue sets in: and this can affect your performance out on the field in a big way.

- Alcohol

Having a single bottle of beer the night before a match or training session is acceptable, particularly if it helps to calm any pre-match nerves you may be experiencing.

But 'over indulging' is perhaps the worst crime you can commit on your body in the run-up to physical exertion. The resulting dehydration can cause slowed reactions, increased risk of injury, a lack of strength and stamina, and decreased performance levels.

A Diet Plan

The diet plan outlined below is simply an exploratory guide to show you how to achieve a balanced diet throughout the week. You may not like some of the ingredients or foods that are listed, and that is fine: simply swap them for something from the same 'family'.

This diet plan provides a combination of complex (slow release) and simple carbohydrates, lean proteins, healthy meal ideas and plenty of opportunities to intake your five portions of fruit and vegetables each day.

Eating right is important, as is eating at the right times. Try and keep your meal times the same each day where possible, as evening meals can be particularly hard to digest and break down when the body is in relaxation mode at night. If you like to go bed at, say, 11 o'clock, then make sure you have eaten your main meal by 8 o'clock at the latest where possible. You can always snack on a muesli bar or fruit in the evenings to keep you ticking over.

This diet plan has been created under the presumption that Saturday is your match day (with Sunday as a recovery day). If your schedule differs from this, then just adjust the days accordingly.

	Monday	Tuesday	Wednesday	Thursday	Friday	Saturday	Sunday
Breakfast	Whole-grain cereal Fruit Fresh Juice	Wholemeal Toast Fruit Green Tea	Porridge with Jam Fresh Juice	Bagel Yoghurt Green Tea	Wholemeal Toast Fruit Fresh Juice	Porridge with Honey Fruit Muesli Bar	Bagel Lean Bacon Grilled Tomatoes Green Tea
Lunch	Grilled Tomatoes On Toast Salad	Grilled Chicken Salad	Tuna Pasta	Spicy Vegetable Noodles	Mackerel Fillets	Chicken Pasta Salad Grilled Vegetables Yoghurt	Scrambled Eggs Low Fat Sausages Wholemeal Toast
Snack	Nuts & Seeds	Smoothie	Yoghurt & Granola	Fruit Nuts & Seeds	Turkey Salad	Smoothie Bagel	Fruit
Dinner	Grilled Fish Sweet Potato Steamed Vegetables	Healthy Pizza Salad	Grilled Chicken Quinoa	Grilled Fish Vegetable Rice	Baked Potato with Beans Salad	Grilled Chicken Steamed Vegetables	Lean Fillet Steak Sweet Potato Fries Salad

Remember, this is merely a guide: feel free to mix up the days and the recipes as you see fit. But you can see the balance on offer, the goodness to be had each day, and the slow building energy releases on match day.

As far as drinks are concerned, remember to drink plenty of water each and every day, and supplement this with isotonic sports drinks on days of activity. Replace tea and coffee with green tea where possible, and remember that fresh fruit smoothies with ice and a tiny bit of low fat milk are both tasty and nutritious.

Chapter 10

Psychology

You might think that training hard, getting in good shape and understanding the game tactically are enough to turn you into a good player. Well, unfortunately, there is another crucial aspect that cannot be overlooked: sports psychology.

There are hundreds of examples of players at all levels throughout the ages who have enjoyed natural talent in abundance. But for those lacking the key psychological components outlined in this chapter, the talent alone was simply not enough for them to carve out a career at the highest level.

Why? Because when the going gets tough, you need to have the right mindset to achieve your goals, otherwise you will simply get found out by opponents who are mentally tougher than you. Your coach may not trust you enough to play you when the pressure is one either. Often in sport, talent alone isn't enough to get the job done.

There are also many examples of players perhaps lacking in natural ability, but who make up for that with a mental toughness that makes them a key component of their team. Roy Keane, of the all-conquering Manchester United team of the late 1990s/early 2000s, is one such example.

There are a few different aspects of psychology that need to be in good condition if you are to achieve your full potential out on the field. Consider each one as a separate entity that combines with the others to create a healthy mindset:

- Confidence

- Concentration

- Composure

- Decision-making

- Winning mentality

- Dealing with setbacks

- Motivation

All of these things are crucial in establishing yourself as a good player; because remember, soccer isn't just played with the feet.

But the good news is that each of these tenets of psychology can be improved and enhanced just like your physical performance can, by exercising them and opening your mind to new ideas.

10.1 - Confidence

It cannot be overestimated how important confidence is to the soccer player's make-up – and it really doesn't matter if you are a pro playing at the highest level or an amateur looking to make your mark in a local league.

Being confident in your own ability is an absolutely fantastic feeling out on the field, and you will find that the more confident you are, the better you will play. Why? It's hard to say: scientists are still unearthing the secrets of the chemical reactions that take place in the brain that creates the sense of confidence. But needless to say, if you feel that you can achieve something then you are far more likely to do so than somebody who doesn't believe that they can do it.

Confidence is not only vital for enhancing your performances, but it is also important in overcoming setbacks and bouncing back from a defeat. All teams lose from time to time, and poor performances happen as well. But the manner in which you take stock, learn from it and use the defeat or poor performance as a positive experience will help you to grow as both a player and a human being.

How is Confidence Measured?

It becomes very clear when a player is suffering from low confidence. They give away many visual and verbal clues, and these are particularly hard to 'cover up' and hide.

The most obvious sign of low confidence is in negative body language. Not wanting to receive the ball, not getting involved in the play, looking disinterested – these are all major signs of low confidence. The player might even look sullen and defeated before they even take to the field.

Another common cause of anxiety and low concentration amongst soccer players is feeling the pressure to live up to the expectations of others; whether that is self-expectation or the need to impress teammates, coaches, friends and family, etc. Feeling pressured in this way has a chronic knock-on effect on confidence.

The consequences of a lack of confidence can be crippling. Imagine a striker, for example, who is lacking in self-belief. The goals will dry up, they will stop trying to execute new skills and instead take the simple option – which may not always be the right call. Attackers who are low on confidence will be terrified of the ball falling to them in the penalty area; he or she will try to 'hide' out on the field. They may be substituted and lose their place in the team. Then it becomes even harder to get that confidence back....

It's a vicious cycle, and as you can see a lack of confidence and self-belief can really separate the good from the great.

So what can be done about it? Well, fortunately you can 'train your brain' to think positively, which in turn breeds confidence. But first it is best to understand which attributes are common amongst confident people, and then see where you can improve on your own weaknesses:

- ✓ Self-belief – 'I CAN do this' being a common theme.

- ✓ Positive body language – relaxed, happy and communicative.

- ✓ No fear of failure – this can significantly damage confidence levels.

- ✓ Live in the moment – take each game as it comes.

- ✓ Play for yourself – with no pressure to impress others.

- ✓ Don't seek perfection – we all make mistakes, live with it.

These are the key psychological aspects that promote confidence. Some occur naturally, some are learnt (i.e. through coaching and interactions), and others can be mastered by yourself.

An easy way of measuring confidence is using this simple equation:

Positive Mindset + Self-belief + Soccer Ability = Confidence = Good Performance

How to Build Confidence

You can bet your bottom dollar that a confident player will outperform one lacking confidence. So how do you become confident? Is it possible to just be confident or is it a process that you have no control over? Can you wake up one morning and your confidence has drained out of you overnight or is it a gradual process?

Anything can knock your confidence, and it really does depend on how highly-strung you are as a personality and how you cope with pressure and failure.

Luckily, you are able to boost your own confidence – and that of your teammates – by taking a few simple steps:

- Encouragement

There's nothing quite like hearing praise when you do something well; maybe you've scored a good goal, put in a great cross or made a well-timed tackle that prevented a dangerous attack.

Hearing praise from coaches and teammates is a wonderful thing, and it's no surprise to learn that the best teams are the ones where an environment of positivity reigns supreme.

- Positive Body Language

Entering the field of play with your chest out and shoulders pulled back, with a bit of a swagger, lets the people around you know that you're feeling positive and confident. This will hopefully rub off on your teammates whilst concerning your opponents, and ultimately this projection – or 'peacocking', as it is known - will also enable you to feel more confident in yourself.

- Calm Under Pressure

There are situations in a match that require a cool head and a composed mind. If you can achieve this, you will instantly instil confidence in your teammates, and they in turn will help you to believe in yourself more. Easier said than done of course, but living in the present will help you to minimise the fear of making mistakes.

- Stay Positive

Many teams ban negative talk and even impose fines for players who are pessimistic in the locker room or out on the field. Although this is a bit extreme, focusing on the positives, no matter what the score of the game is or how good your opponents are, can help with your confidence.

You may remember the legendary Muhammad Ali's 'I am the Greatest' speech prior to his win over Sonny Liston all those years ago. Ali was a huge underdog in that encounter, but that speech proved that not only did he not fear Liston, he was absolutely convinced that he would win – even telling his opponent which round the fight would end in!

Now, whilst I'm not suggesting you go to those extreme lengths, just remind yourself and your teammates that soccer is a game played by two teams of eleven with a round leather ball. There's no complexity to it, no mystery....just get out on the field and play your natural game. If you work hard enough, you will be rewarded.

- Turn Negatives Into Positives

All players, no matter what their level of ability, will feel negative and nervous at times. The ones who can identify these pessimistic thoughts and use their energy to turn these into a positive are the ones who rise above the rest.

'What if I miss an open goal' can easily become 'I'm getting into good positions'.

'What if I lose the player I'm supposed to be marking' can easily become 'I'm going to make sure I don't lose my focus for the next 90 minutes'.

'I'm nervous' can easily become 'I'm nervous – this means I'm motivated to do well'.

That is the kind of thought process you must go through if you are to turn negative energy into positive. Having this mindset is vital in maintaining confidence in soccer and life in general.

- Believe in Yourself/Affirmative Visualisation

Can you remember when you scored that great goal in training the other day? What about the time you made that brilliant tackle/cross/defense-splitting pass? You see, you are capable of achieving fantastic things out on the field – no matter how low in confidence you are right now.

It is positive visualisation like this, of reminding yourself what you are truly capable of, that fires self-belief, and self-belief is what fires confidence. Simple really!

Remember, success breeds success, and this positive confidence cycle is important in developing a strong psychological framework on which to call when things really do get tough.

- Preparation

Training hard for your match will help you to feel prepared, and that feeling of preparedness can be the 'marginal gain' that can distinguish a good performance from a bad one, and, as such, a win from a loss. Each individual has their own method of feeling prepared: whether it is a physical preparation – maybe lifting some weights or going for a jog, or mental preparation such as walking through your role and the match itself in your mind. Once you get into a routine of preparing effectively, it will become second nature.

Of course, giving yourself the best possible opportunity to perform is the very best preparation. Eating well and drinking lots of water will help to prepare your body for the big match, and you will feel full of confidence if you have taken these steps. And don't be afraid to watch a teammate or a player on the television to see how they go about their business; this can give you a great sense of purpose. If you can capture video footage of yourself, and put together a highlights reel of your greatest goals/passes/tackles/saves, then you will be walking on air!

- Play To Your Strengths

We'd all like to be able to ping 40-yard passes across the field or score bicycle kicks from the edge of the penalty area, but frankly only the select few are capable of very special feats like that.

Instead, you should stick to what you are good at and play to your strengths: knowing where you excel is a great confidence booster!

Top Tip:

✓ Psychological hack to build confidence: Around 10 minutes before a match starts, try to remember and visualize your best moments in previous matches or training sessions; your best shots, best movements, best tackles, best passes, etc. Now take those memories, and imagine you doing them in the match you're about to play. Hopefully, this hack will instill the confidence you need to perform to your highest level.

10.2 - Composure & Decision-Making

Soccer, by its very nature, is a fast and furious sport. It doesn't matter what level of the game you are at, the speed in which you have to play and make decisions is incredible; from spotting clever runs and defense-splitting passes, to the time it takes your brain to register that the other team is about to embark on a dangerous counter-attack and you'd better help your defense out pronto.

The relative time it takes for you to make such decisions is based not only on your prowess for decision-making but also on your composure. The Oxford English Dictionary definition of composure is 'the state or feeling of being calm and in control of oneself.' As you can imagine then, being composed out on the field can have great benefit to your decision-making and your ability to perform under pressure.

Composure is a skill needed in abundance by strikers, who often find themselves through on goal with just the keeper to beat. Remaining composed when the chance of scoring presents itself – particularly when it would be an important goal in the context of the match – is invaluable. As it is when taking a penalty, or indeed if you are playing in goal and facing a spot kick.

But it is important for defenders to remain composed when timing tackles too, and midfielders when finding that killer pass or pinpoint cross. Basically, composure is a great asset for any player, no matter what position they play in.

Like many psychological aspects of the game, some people are more naturally composed than others, but that's not to say that composure levels cannot be improved with practice and 'exercise'.

How to Improve Composure

Composure is governed by the amount of adrenaline coursing through your veins at any given time: too much of it and you might be prone to rash decisions or missing opportunities, whereas those who are known to be 'ice cold' and calm under pressure can make magic happen from out of nowhere.

So how can you improve your composure?

- Feeling Relaxed

We often hear about being 'psyched up' before a match, and it's true that a certain amount of adrenaline can be a good thing.

But in reality, it is far better to be calm and relaxed over agitated and restless, as you can burn off a lot of energy through nervousness. Your ability to think clearly is affected too, so take all of the steps you can to remain calm and collected before stepping out onto the field.

Practising calming exercises before a match or training will be a great help; many top players will sit in a state of complete silence and calm before a game, and simply practise breathing slowly and rhythmically to bring their heart rate levels down. Some will listen to music on an MP3 player to block out the buzz around them. These tactics can help to 'trick' the brain into feelings of composure and complete calm; despite the nerves you might actually be feeling.

- Think Ahead

Try and become so comfortable in your role that you know what to do before the ball comes to you. If you have an idea of where the space is and where your teammates are, then you can prepare to deliver the most effective pass almost instinctively. Do you want to play one touch to a close teammate, do you want to turn into space, or do you want to play a long pass into space for a dangerously placed colleague? Having a map of the field in your mind, and thinking ahead, is crucial for players in all positions.

Whilst forward thinking in soccer is manifested in strong positional sense and reading the game, possessing strong technical abilities will also help you to make the most of your limited time on the ball. Making the right choices is one thing, actually carrying them out is quite another. So work on your close control and passing abilities, as this will give you a significant amount of more time on the ball. And try and think a couple of passes ahead: once you have delivered the ball to a teammate, where do you need to be next? Or are you going to sprint into space or hold your position? Staying one step ahead of the opposition is one of the key drivers of success out on the field.

- Confidence and Focus

If you believe in yourself and are confident of success, then naturally you will be more composed than those who fear failure and worry about making mistakes. Instead, you need to program your brain to believe that winning and performing well are automatic as soon as you step onto the field.

And this is linked to focus, of existing 'in the moment' and letting events unfold in front of you. Simply focus on your goals and then let your natural talent take over.

- The Autopilot

The Autopilot takes over when you're feeling good about your game. Everything becomes automatic – passes, shot, crosses, tackles – you can perform all of these without even thinking.

This is the perfect psychological state for any athlete because The Autopilot has no problem with keeping composure! When decision-making is natural and effortless, you are able to play the beautiful game without emotion clouding your judgement.

How to Improve Decision-Making

Did you know that the average player spends less than three minutes on the ball during any one given match? When you think about it like that, it's obvious why good decision-making is so important. You only have a limited time-frame to make your mark, and making a good decision at the right time can be the difference between success and failure.

Despite decision-making being an instinctive emotion, rather than a tangible skill, it can be hard to improve it outright. But by changing the way you think about the game, and putting in the work off the field, you should notice that you begin to make the right decision in a match more often than not.

- Practice makes Perfect

Repetition breeds confidence when the time comes to make a split-second decision, and as such the importance of practice cannot be overstated. This will help to ensure that the game becomes second nature to you – which naturally aids effective decision-making.

- Work on your Ball Control

Good decision-making is all about buying yourself more time to make the right judgment call. By practising your ball control in particular you are giving yourself the perfect chance to create more time and space.

- Think of Soccer as a Game of Chess

All of the great chess masters think at least two plays ahead of where the game is at any given moment. So if you can see a few passages of play ahead in soccer – if you can see an early pass, an empty pocket of space to run into or a dangerous attack building – then your decision-making process will be made all the more easier.

- Be Tactically Aware

By understanding your particular role on the field better, you should be able to make effective decisions that increase the likelihood of you being in the right place at the right time. Make sure you fully understand your role by talking to your coach should you need to, and don't forget to watch your favourite players closely for a great insight into your ideal positioning.

- Keep it Simple

The biggest handicap to good decision-making is over-elaboration. It's the players who try to do too much with the ball or attempt the impossible, for whom bad decisions are a problem. Instead, just keep things simple and retain possession; this makes the whole decision-making process a heck of a lot easier! You can only score if you've got the ball, and you will make yourself far more valuable to your team if you're renowned for maintaining possession.

10.3 - Focus and Concentration

Mistakes can happen all the time in soccer, that's just the nature of this fast-paced sport, but it's interesting to see just how many errors can be avoided. Whether it's a striker missing a golden opportunity to score or a defender giving the ball away in their own half, so many mistakes can be put down to 'human error' as to bad luck or misfortune.

One of the main factors that creates mistakes out on the field is a loss of concentration and focus. As mentioned before, soccer is such a fast-paced, 'blink of the eye' sport that even taking your eye off the ball for a second can be catastrophic.

It can be hard to concentrate for a full 90 minutes without losing focus every once in a while, especially when there are so many things going on. But there is a technique called 'selective attention' which gives you the opportunity to take a break from intense concentration for a moment in order to avoid mental fatigue.

You can also use breaks in play, such as when the ball is kicked out for a throw-in or a player is injured and receiving treatment, to enjoy a forced break in concentration. This is a useful strategy if you make sure you are back to being fully focused once the game resumes!

Selective Attention

Imagine playing a game where 100 balls of various colours were fired at you from a machine, and your goal was to only catch balls of a certain colour. This, in a fashion, explains the skill of selective attention.

When you have hundreds of stimuli going on around you at any one time, it is focusing on one single object amongst these – whilst isolating the rest - that forms the basis of selective attention. This is a conscious effort of course, and relies on us as individuals to focus on the selected stimuli above all others.

In a soccer context, selective attention is focusing solely on the match – and nothing else. Whatever is going on in your personal life, whoever is standing on the sidelines cheering you on...these things are, for the time you are on the field, irrelevant.

Your only focus should be on the role you are undertaking in your team. Because one break in concentration can turn a win into a draw, a draw into a loss....and, of course, your teammates will be devastated by that.

In many ways, improving your concentration skills through a model like selective attention is almost as important as practicing your passing, shooting or tactical role. It can greatly enhance your abilities as a soccer player, and make you a more desirable player to pick over somebody who lacks mental sharpness and focus.

As mentioned before, soccer is a sport played principally with the feet....and the brain.

What Causes a Lack of Concentration?

There are a number of causes of lapses in concentration, with each individual prone to one more than others. Of course, a lack of concentration is loosely defined as 'the mind being elsewhere other than the present', and this can be caused by any number of factors.

This can be personal problems; again if you are having issues off the field with money, jobs, partners, etc, then this can have a knock-on effect to your performances on the field. This is where selective attention once again comes in handy.

And then there are the on-field factors which can impact upon concentration levels. For defenders and goalkeepers, maintaining focus can be difficult if they aren't kept busy (if their teammates are dominating possession for example). Often, in tight games, strikers get one chance and one chance only to break the deadlock too: so being prepared and focused is a necessity.

The classic syndrome is 'ball watching', which is where a player focuses on the ball rather than keeping an eye on the movements of an opponent or to where they should be positioning themselves on the field. So the key is to focus on your job, rather than following the ball. If that role is to closely mark an opponent then that must be your primary aim.

Remember, a weakness in the psychological aspects of soccer can prevent you from progressing further in the game, and these should be worked on in as much detail as the physical parts of the sport.

The six key problems caused by a loss in concentration:

1. Opponents left unmarked

2. Sloppy passing/giving away the ball

3. Poor decision-making

4. Poor first touch

5. Delayed reactions

6. Below par movement into space

How to Improve Concentration

Concentration is not necessarily a skill we are born with; some of us need to work hard at improving our focus. This begins on the training field – you should treat each session as if it was a match, in order to help 'train your brain'. The time for fun and socialising with teammates is after the job is done.

The next time you have a match-type situation in a training session, make sure you focus and bring the same intensity as you would in a proper game. Remember your roles and responsibilities, keep things simple, don't talk to your opponents about casual topics (you wouldn't do that in a game!) and, lastly, do everything in your power to win the training match.

Remember, the brain is a muscle that needs flexing just as much as any other. You will notice that your concentration levels improve if you adopt a kind of 'on/off switch' in your brain that is activated and deactivated by playing soccer – whether an actual match or just training. Getting used to doing so in a non-pressurised environment will undoubtedly help you in the real thing.

So to improve concentration you must:

• Establish Professional/Personal Barriers

There will be plenty of time to chat about the weekend and the world of soccer after the game/training; first you need to focus on the task in hand. Your teammates will respect you for this approach.

- Set Achievable Goals

By giving yourself explicit targets, you should remain focused until they have been achieved. If you still find yourself losing concentration, then perhaps your goals are too easy/too hard to accomplish. Remember to tick off your steps towards your objectives as well.

- Know your Role

'Fail to prepare, prepare to fail.' That's an old saying that still runs as true today as the day that former US president Benjamin Franklin said it. So make sure you know your position and your duties on the field inside and out, and use these in your goal setting as outlined above.

- Live in the Moment

Forget about everything that is not important to you winning the match. Things that are going on in your life away from the field are irrelevant. Whatever happened in your last match is now gone. Focus solely on the matter at hand and you won't go far wrong. The next cross, the next pass, the next tackle; they are all that matter right now.

- Stay Positive

Forget about that missed chance or the yellow card, that doesn't matter now. Focus on what you can bring to the rest of the match or training session instead. Negative thoughts need to be isolated as unhelpful, because what you do now is what really counts. Remember your goals and make them happen.

- Verbal Reinforcement

A good trigger to remain focused at all times is to recite some keywords or phrases. These act as a reminder to keep switched on and remain alert to any danger, as well as reminding you of your role within the team. Have a couple of stock phrases prepared to help keep your head in the game.

- Switch Off and Relax

Concentrating fully for 90 minutes can be exhausting. So you need to teach yourself to switch off and relax at opportune moments in matches. If the game is stopped for an injury, or the ball has kicked out for a goal kick, then take the moment to take a breather. As soon as the referee blows the whistle to restart the game then switch back on.

10.4 - Winning and Losing

It's a funny thing in sport, but it's apparent that both winning and losing can become a habit. Teams that are used to winning find a way to win close matches or those where they are on the back foot for the majority of the game.

Likewise, teams that make a habit of losing can develop a fear of winning, and can throw away matches when most of the hard work is done. That debilitating dread at the prospect of getting over the winning line is one of the most incapacitating conditions in both individual and team sports.

The Losing Mentality

It's not always easy to stay positive when embroiled in a losing streak, but it pays to do so as teams that stick together tend to do much better than those who resort to in-fighting, arguing and pointing the finger of blame at certain individuals.

We tend to look at things in black and white in life, but in soccer there are often shades of grey. How many times have you seen the better team lose in a match? That's just the sport, and you need to reconcile yourself with that fact.

So if you find yourselves becoming the victim of a losing mentality, ask yourself this: did we deserve to lose today, based on how hard we worked and the chances we created? If the answer is yes then sure; there is likely to be hard work ahead. If the answer is no, then stick to what you're doing as a win is surely just around the corner.

Some coaches insist on calling it winning and learning, rather than winning and losing, so maybe take this philosophy on board too. We can all learn things in defeat, regroup and then move on to the next match. In this sense, you now have two positive potential outcomes rather than a single positive or a negative.

The Winning Mentality

Of course, it's much nicer to be on the winning side, and so building a positive mindset is invaluable. Once positivity runs through a club, it is often followed by success on the field.

The happiest teams are the ones that get along off the field as well as on it, and again that's where the social element is so important. Building friendships and making being part of the club fun and something to look forward to rather than dread is important, and it's no surprise to learn that sides who have players who are willing to run through metaphorical brick walls for their teammates are usually the most successful.

Pulling together to achieve the same goals helps, so make sure that your team has a collective objective as well as your own individual targets. By working together you and your teammates can achieve great things.

How else can you create a winning mindset?

- Freedom of Expression

For individuals to really flourish they need to know that they can play with complete freedom, rather than the fear of being reprimanded by a teammate or coach if they try something that doesn't quite work. So play your part in nurturing a creative environment by encouraging your fellow players to express themselves on the field.

- Face up to Adversity

Every dog has its day, and so you can't expect to win every game. A good winning mentality is a bond that isn't shattered by one bad result; and adversity should bring out the best in people. So investigate why you lost but don't dwell on it, and prepare twice as hard for the next match.

- Set Realistic Goals

We'd all like to win the league, but in truth only one team can secure that accolade. Instead, write down a desired result you'd love to achieve against each fixture in your calendar. Remind your teammates that 'we can win today' if you are the stronger team, but do so in a way that doesn't invite pressure.

If you are playing against a stronger team, remind your teammates that you can still get a good result if you work hard and stick to your tactics. Sometimes taking the pressure off can work wonders for peoples' confidence.

- Lead from the Front

Some people like to lead; others like to be led. If you play in a team that is short of natural leaders, then why don't you take up the baton? You may not think of yourself as a natural leader, but you can still achieve results without shouting from the rooftops. Remind players of their goals, and remember how good the euphoria of winning feels.

- Stick at it

Rome wasn't built in a day, so make sure you don't get too disheartened after a couple of negative results. It takes time to build a winning mindset, but as long as you are working hard and together as a team then your time will come.

10.5 - Motivation

What are your reasons for playing soccer?

Do you love the sport? Do you enjoy the camaraderie with your teammates? Maybe you enjoy the exercise? Or perhaps you want to become the best player?

Your reasons for playing are ultimately your motivation for taking the time and effort to get to training, to eat well and to prepare for your matches. A lack of motivation will more often than not lead to a poor performance, so understanding your own reasons for playing are necessary in remaining motivated and giving yourself the best chance you can of raising your game.

Motivation comes from within; it is a psychological process that leads to a physical action, and finding it is important, not just for playing well but also in preparing for your matches. You need to be:

- Motivated to train and work on your skills.

- Motivated to understand your position in the team and its tactics.

- Motivated to push yourself the extra yard in matches.

- Motivated to eat well and stick to your healthy eating plan.

The Main Challenges to Motivation

1. Losing Matches

All teams go through bad patches every once in a while, and finding the motivation to help your team through this run is crucial.

Solution: Remember the good times, that euphoric feeling of winning and being successful. Remember that your teammates are hurting too, and you need to all pull together to turn things around. An extra 10% of effort in training and in matches can make all the difference.

2. Personal Problems

We all suffer from off-the-field problems from time to time, whether it is money issues, heartbreak or boredom with our jobs. Sometimes we can take these problems onto the field of play with us, and that can affect our motivation to really involve ourselves in the game when our minds are elsewhere.

Solution: Isolate your personal problems from your soccer, and don't take out any surplus aggression on your opponents. Remember, soccer can be a great way to forget about your problems, so fully invest yourself in the match and forget about your issues for 90 minutes at least!

3. Being Played Out of Position

Sometimes, your coach might not play you in the position you want to play in. That can be incredibly demoralising, particularly when you have worked very hard to make the place your own.

Solution: Have a talk with your coach as to why they are playing you in a different position: perhaps he or she sees something in you? Maybe they really value your versatility? Or it could be a tactical decision for this one match?

4. Not Playing

It's the worst feeling in the world: being told you are not in the starting eleven. Even the best players in the world face a spell on the sidelines, but that doesn't make it any easier to take. You may be feeling that the world is against you – which is not a very motivating emotion.

Solution: Be patient, work hard to improve your game, and your chance will come.

5. Not Enjoying Training

Everybody gets to a point when they don't enjoy their training – it could be cold or rainy outside, or maybe your coach's training methods aren't to your liking. Your performance level can affect motivation levels too: if you are playing poorly, the last thing you may want to do is go back out on the training field.

Solution: The key to getting the enjoyment out of training is visualisation. Visualising the rewards you will enjoy in your game from training hard and working on your skills can be a great way to motivate yourself; what do you want to achieve in the sport? Whatever it is, it will undoubtedly require hard work to make it happen. So when training loses its enjoyment, think of your ultimate objectives.

Motivation Tips and Techniques

To better understand how you can motivate yourself to achieve bigger and better things, you first must appreciate that there are two unique types of motivation:

Intrinsic – a personal motivation to succeed

Extrinsic – motivation from others (coaches, teammates, friends, etc)

By breaking the notion of motivation down into these two distinct parts, you can see that you as an individual have a key role to play in motivating yourself – you can't always expect others simply to do the job for you.

From a personal perspective, you really need to define what you want to achieve from your soccer:

- Goal Setting

What is realistic? Do you want to score 25 goals a season? Keep 10 clean sheets? Create 3 chances per game for your teammates? Or simply have fun, enjoy yourself and get fit? The level of goals you set for yourself, and its difficulty to achieve, will help to determine your own intrinsic motivation level.

- The Need to Achieve

We all have a need to achieve things in our life and to get recognition from our peers for our achievements. This is intrinsic motivation in itself then, although we all have differing levels of 'self actualisation' that need satisfying.

But the need to win matches, score goals, make tackles and win trophies is evident in all of us; yet it is only those who are motivated to put the hard work in that will achieve their ambitions.

- Personality

We're all different as people of course, and personality can play a huge part in determining the individual's motivation levels. For some more laidback characters, motivation can often be hard to come by, whilst more assertive and passionate people are motivated easily by a wealth of factors, with their desire to succeed very much an intrinsic part of their everyday lives.

As you'd expect, it is the more motivated player that tends to go on to achieve great things, but that's not to say that less intrinsically motivated individuals are doomed to failure. The key is in your goal setting – what do you want to achieve? Why? And what do you need to do to accomplish this feat? As long as you have some kind of overriding ambition to fulfil, then you will remain motivated to succeed.

Extrinsic Motivation

As you might expect, playing for a team that is very vocal in its motivation for one another is hugely important. If you are playing for a team where the environment is very insular and selfish, then you will struggle to find the motivation to want to go through the whole 'blood, sweat and tears' thing for your teammates.

And this is why extrinsic motivation is important: because sometimes our own self-motivation simply isn't enough. We need to feel the need to achieve on behalf of others, to bring joy and success to our fellow players and coaches through our individual actions.

Enjoying an environment where coaches and players support one another, are quick with praise when things go well, and are happy to encourage when things do not, will help to motivate you as an individual - and the importance of this should not be overlooked. Ask yourself if the environment in your team's dressing room is positive and constructive if you find yourself lacking in motivation.

How to Motivate Yourself

Really, motivation does differ from individual to individual, but there are common principles you can follow. Once you've unearthed your motivation for playing the beautiful game, then you can learn how to motivate yourself to achieve your objectives.

Some of the ideas outlined below won't be relevant to everybody, but each can help you to find that extra percentage to really make the most of your ability.

- Ever-Changing Training Plans

It's no secret that repetition is the worst enemy of motivation, and that is especially true of training. If you're doing the same training drills and exercises over and over again, finding the motivation to train can be extremely difficult.

And this is why an ever-changing training plan that is interesting and fulfilling is so important. This will keep you motivated to get out onto the field, whilst helping you to improve both physically and technically.

Your training should be both mentally and physically stimulating, and should never feel like a chore. Enjoying your training is the only way to gain anything from it.

- Goal Setting/Progress Tracking

You've got to have something to aim towards as a soccer player. Setting yourself some realistic goals that are relevant to your position is crucial, as is monitoring your progress towards achieving them.

The goal must be attractive and achievable – if it isn't, then your motivation to accomplish it will be non-existent. But if it is too easy then where is the motivation to realize it? So think about what is relevant and achievable.

You can measure this in steps by 'ticking off' accomplishments en route to the overall goal. This will keep you motivated at all times rather than periodically, and gives you a visual aid as to your successes so far.

And don't forget to reward yourself for achieving your steps. Whether it's a special purchase or even a day off from your diet plan, your reward should be something that really gets your juices flowing!

- Watch Your Heroes

Fewer things can be more motivating than watching your favourite players in action. Whilst it might be unrealistic to think that you can emulate the likes of Lionel Messi in terms of their achievements, you can learn so much by watching their movement, their technique and how they approach the game.

Watching Messi or Cristiano Ronaldo dribble the ball past three defenders before slamming a shot into the top corner is incredibly motivating. With practise and hard work, sticking to a healthy diet and working on the psychological aspects of the game, maybe you can have the same impact on your team as those two greats of the modern game.

Knowing that some of the world's best players came from the most humble backgrounds is also a motivating factor.

- Help to Build Team Unity

It's no secret that intrinsic and extrinsic motivation are inextricably linked: developing a bond with your teammates on a personal level will motivate you personally to want to win for them just as much as yourself.

So building team unity is important, and you can achieve this by spending some quality time in each other's' company away from the soccer field. Try and make a connection and establish some common ground, because once you have some shared experiences it is easier to see things from other peoples' perspectives if you have a disagreement about tactics, training drills, etc.

A winning team is one that gets along and pulls together when things get tough. You will find yourself to be extra motivated individually if your team is motivated collectively.

10 Motivational Quotes from the Pro's

Still struggling to get motivated? Then maybe you need to change your mindset a little. Being positive and achieving everything you want to achieve is down to skill, luck, hard work, preparation and a will to win.

All of the legends of the game have had to find their own motivation from somewhere. If you are struggling to find the motivation to train or eat right, then maybe the words of the likes of Pele and some other greats will have the desired effect:

"Success is no accident. It is hard work, perseverance, learning, studying, sacrifice and most of all, love of what you are doing or learning to do." **Pele**

"What kind of a goalkeeper is the one who is not tormented by the goal he has allowed? He must be tormented! And if he is calm, that means the end. No matter what he had in the past, he has no future." **Lev Yashin**

"I don't believe skill was, or ever will be, the result of coaches. It is a result of a love affair between the child and the ball." **Roy Keane**

"Failure happens all the time. It happens every day in practice. What makes you better is how you react to it." – **Mia Hamm**

"A lot of football success is in the mind. You must believe that you are the best and then make sure that you are." – **Bill Shankly**

"When you win, you don't get carried away. But if you go step by step, with confidence, you can go far." – **Diego Maradona**

"If you do not believe you can do it then you have no chance at all." – **Arsene Wenger**

"For sportsmen or women who want to be champions, the mind can be as important, if not more important, than any other part of the body." - **Gary Neville**

"Every disadvantage has its advantage." - **Johan Cruyff**

"You only stop learning when you quit." - **Ruud Gullit**

Chapter 11

Your Soccer Performance

Now is the chance for you to evaluate your own soccer performance. The attributes you are about to mark yourself on represent your skills and abilities. The result of marking your own attributes is for you to find out what your strengths and weaknesses are. This will allow you to improve your overall game attribute by attribute (and perhaps get you to work on a few of the sometimes neglected psychological attributes).

When giving yourself a rating, think about your overall performance in your last 10 – 20 matches (or training sessions) – this should give you a consistent mark. Also keep in mind the level you're playing at. It's best to compare yourself to other players in the same team or in the same league, because if you compare yourself to someone who is on a much higher level than you, it can be hard to measure your true ability.

Using a PENCIL, mark yourself out of 20 for each attribute, with 1 being very poor and 20 being almost perfect. Each attribute has a set of questions underneath to give you a better understanding, the chapters that will help you improve the attribute, and the positions that are most related to the attribute. The positions have been shortened to the following:

GK = Goalkeeper

CB = Center Back

FB = Fullback (or Wingback)

DM = Defensive Midfielder

CM = Center Midfielder

AM = Winger + Attacking Midfielder

F= Forward

Try to mark yourself as honestly as possible (you can even ask your coach to help) as the end goal is to improve yourself as a player. Once you feel you have improved an attribute and are able to consistently play to that standard, erase your mark and give yourself a new rating.

11.1 - Technical

Ball Control (First Touch)   *GK – CB – FB – DM – CM – AM – F*

How good is your first touch when receiving the ball from different heights and speeds? How well can you control the ball with various parts of your body (head, chest, knee, feet, etc.)? How good is your touch direction?

Chapters: 1.1

20

Technique   *GK – CB – FB – DM – CM – AM – F*

How well do you execute your passes, shots, headers and dribbling? Are you conscious of body position, body shape, part of the foot/head being used, where you strike the ball, and the amount of power and accuracy you are placing into the technique?

Chapters: 1 - 1.9

20

Predictability   *CB – FB – DM – CM – AM – F*

How well can you disguise your movements? E.g. movement into space, forward runs, dribbling. How well can you disguise your touch direction when receiving the ball and when playing a pass to a teammate? Can opposition players regularly predict your movements and intentions?

Chapters: 1.9, 3.2 & 4.1

20

Keeping Possession   *GK – CB – FB – DM – CM – AM – F*

Do you often give the ball away unnecessarily? Do you always try to make yourself available and ready to receive a pass? How good are you at shielding the ball from opponents?

Chapters: 1.3, 2.3 & 4.1

20

Short Pass   *GK – CB – FB – DM – CM – AM – F*

How accurate are your short passes? Do you have a high short pass completion rate? How often do you under-hit or over-hit your short passes?

Chapters: 1.2 & 1.3

20

Long Pass   *GK – CB – FB – DM – CM – AM – F*

How accurate are your long passes? Do you have a high long pass completion rate? How often do you under-hit or over-hit your long passes?

Chapters: 1.2 & 1.3

20

Volleying   *CB – FB – DM – CM – AM – F*

How good is your volleying timing and technique? How accurate are your volleys?

Chapters: 1.2 & 1.6

20

Dribbling   *CB – FB – DM – CM – AM – F*

How well do you control the ball while running with it? How good are your dribbling skills?
How good are you at dribbling past opponents?

Chapters: 1.4

20

Heading   *CB – FB – DM – CM – AM – F*

How accurate are your headers? How powerful are your headers? How often do you win headers
you challenge for?

Chapters: 1.7

20

Weaker Foot   *GK – CB – FB – DM – CM – AM – F*

Can you use your weaker foot with confidence? How accurate is your weaker foot when
shooting and passing? How powerful is your weaker foot when shooting? How good is your
technique with your weaker foot when dribbling and passing?

Chapters: 1 – 1.9

20

Creativity   *FB – DM – CM – AM – F*

How good is your ability in creating attacking and goal scoring opportunities? How often do you
create attacking and goal scoring opportunities?

Chapters: 1.3, 1.4, 1.9 & 3.1

20

Through Balls   *DM – CM – AM – F*

How accurate are your short and long through balls? How often do you under-hit or over-hit
your through balls? Do your through balls always find their intended targets?

Chapters: 1.2 & 1.3

20

Crossing   *FB – CM – AM – F*

How often do your crosses find their intended targets? Are you able to consistently put your
crosses in dangerous areas with pace and precision?

Chapters: 1.2 & 1.8

20

Shooting Accuracy   *CM – AM – F*

Do you regularly find the target using different shooting techniques? How accurate are your shots from different angles and ranges? Do you have a high shot/goal ratio?

Chapters: 1.2 & 1.6

20

Shooting Power   *DM – CM – AM – F*

How powerful are your shots? Are you able to generate a lot of power with different shooting techniques? Are you able to consistently hit the target while shooting as hard as you can?

Chapters: 1.2 & 1.6

20

Long Range Shooting   *DM – CM – AM – F*

When shooting from outside the box, how accurately and powerfully can you shoot at your intended target? Are you able to regularly find the corner of the goal when shooting from outside the box?

Chapters: 1.2, 1.6 & 4.1

20

Tackling   *CB – FB – DM – CM – AM*

How well can you take the ball from your opponent without committing a foul? Are you able to use a range of tackling techniques? How well do you time your tackles? How good are your slide tackles?

Chapters: 1.5

20

Jockeying   *CB – FB – DM – CM – AM*

How well can you contain an opponent? How well can you force an opponent (with the ball) away from the danger areas?

Chapters: 1.5

20

Interceptions   *CB – FB – DM – CM – AM*

How well can you predict where the opposition intend to pass the ball? How quickly can you react to a potential interception?

Chapters: 1.5

20

Marking   *CB – FB – DM – CM*

How well do you man or zonal mark an opponent on set pieces? How well do you man or zonal mark an opponent in open play?

Chapters: 1.5 & 7.2

20

11.2 - Tactical

Communication   *GK – CB – FB – DM – CM – AM – F*

How good are your verbal and visual communication skills? Do you know the main soccer phrases and gestures and what they mean? Do you communicate with your teammates at the right times?

Chapters: 2.7, 5, 5.1 & 6.1

20

Movement   *CB – FB – DM – CM – AM – F*

When your team are in possession, how good are you at finding space, giving your teammates a passing option, or creating space for teammates to exploit? How well do you time your movements?

Chapters: 3.1, 3.2, 4.1 & 4.2

20

Positioning   *GK – CB – FB – DM – CM – AM – F*

How well do you move and position yourself when your team don't have possession and when dealing with an opposition attack?

Chapters: 4.1, 4.2, 5 – 5.2 & 6.1(GK)

20

Teamwork   *CB – FB – DM – CM – AM – F*

How well do you work with your teammates? Do you tend to make selfish decisions?

Chapters: 2 – 2.7, 4.2 & 5 – 5.2

20

Tactical Awareness   *GK – CB – FB – DM – CM – AM – F*

How good are you at reading your opponent's' strengths and exploiting their weaknesses? How well do you follow tactical instructions? How often are you caught out of position?

Chapters: 2 – 2.8, 3.2, 4.2 & 5 – 5.2

20

11.3 - Psychological

Confidence   *GK – CB – FB – DM – CM – AM – F*

How much belief do you have in your own ability? Are you able to maintain your confidence or does it fluctuate? Do you get easily intimidated by your opponents?

Chapters: 6.1 & 10.1

20

Composure
GK – CB – FB – DM – CM – AM – F

Are you able to stay calm and think things through when in possession of the ball? How composed are you when under pressure? Do you ever panic in situations during a match?

Chapters: 3.2, 5 & 10.2

$$\frac{}{20}$$

Concentration
GK – CB – FB – DM – CM – AM – F

How often do you lose your concentration in a match? E.g. lose possession unnecessarily, leave your opponent unmarked, poor first touch, etc. Are you able to maintain focus as you tire throughout a match?

Chapters: 5, 5.1 & 10.3

$$\frac{}{20}$$

Awareness
GK – CB – FB – DM – CM – AM – F

How aware are you of the movements and actions of your teammates and opponents? How good is your spatial awareness? Do you know where your teammates and opponents are at all times?

Chapters: 3.1, 4.1, 4.1 & 5 – 5.2

$$\frac{}{20}$$

Anticipation
GK – CB – FB – DM – CM – AM – F

How well can you predict movements and actions of your teammates and opponents? How quickly do you react to movements and actions of your teammates and opponents? How good are you at staying onside when running for a through ball? How good are you at staying in line with your teammates when playing the offside trap?

Chapters: 3.1, 3.2, 4.1 & 5 – 5.2

$$\frac{}{20}$$

Vision
CB – FB – DM – CM – AM – F

How well can you see the options available to you when on the ball or just about to receive the ball? How well can you identify potential attacking opportunities? E.g. players in space, runs in behind

Chapters: 3.1

$$\frac{}{20}$$

Decision-Making
GK – CB – FB – DM – CM – AM – F

How quickly can you assess the options you are aware of when on and off the ball? How quickly can you evaluate what action to take, and when and how to perform it? Are the majority of your decisions effective?

Chapters: 3.1, 4.2, 6.1(GK) & 10.2

$$\frac{}{20}$$

Determination
GK – CB – FB – DM – CM – AM – F

How determined are you to win every match? How determined are you in trying to succeed in your actions? E.g. win tackles, dribble past a player, win a header, etc. If you fail in an action, how determined are you to make amends?

Chapters: 3.2 & 10.4

20

Discipline
GK – CB – FB – DM – CM – AM – F

How often do you get unnecessary yellow and red cards? Are you often involved in conflict with opponents or teammates? How often do you ignore instructions, tactics, and strategies?

Chapters: 10 – 10.5

20

Work Rate
CB – FB – DM – CM – AM – F

How much effort do you put in during a match?

Chapters: 3.1, 8.1 & 10.4

20

Controlled Aggression
GK – CB – FB – DM – CM – AM – F

How aggressive are you when competing with an opponent for the ball? How often do you choose to get involved in a physical situation? E.g. tackling, marking. Do you tend to get overly aggressive? Are you able to assert yourself without performing an illegal move? E.g. foul, pulling an opponent's shirt, losing your temper, etc.

Chapters: 1.5 & 5.1

20

Bravery
GK – CB – FB – DM – CM – AM – F

How willing are you to perform an action that might cause pain or injury? E.g. going for a header or a tackle. Do you ever shy away from a challenge?

Chapters: 5.1 & 10.1

20

Adaptability
GK – CB – FB – DM – CM – AM – F

How well do you adjust to different weather and field conditions? Are you able to play in a range of different formations? Can you play in more than one role and position?

Chapters: 2.1, 2.2, 4.1 & 9.1

20

Consistency
GK – CB – FB – DM – CM – AM – F

How consistent are your performances on the field?

Chapters: 10 – 10.5 & 9 – 9.3

20

Motivation
GK – CB – FB – DM – CM – AM – F

How easily do you lose motivation? How well are you able to re-motivate yourself after a setback such as losing a match or losing your place in the first team? Do you know what provides you with motivation?

Chapters: 10.5

$$\overline{20}$$

Winning Mentality
GK – CB – FB – DM – CM – AM – F

Do you go into every game thinking your team can win? Do you have a positive mentality? How much do you push yourself to try to win every match?

Chapters: 10.1 & 10.4

$$\overline{20}$$

11.4 - Physical

Balance
GK – CB – FB – DM – CM – AM – F

How well do you maintain your stability when twisting, turning, accelerating and decelerating? How well do you maintain your balance when dribbling, controlling, passing and shooting the ball?

Chapters: 8.2, 8.3 & 8.4

$$\overline{20}$$

Acceleration
GK – CB – FB – DM – CM – AM – F

How fast can you accelerate over 5, 15, and 30 yards compared to other players? Can you get off the mark quicker than opponents in a foot race?

Chapters: 1.4, 8.3 & 8.4

$$\overline{20}$$

Speed
GK – CB – FB – DM – CM – AM – F

How fast can you run 75 yards (or 70 meters)?

Chapters: 8.3 & 8.4

$$\overline{20}$$

Speed endurance
CB – FB – DM – CM – AM – F

How long can you maintain near-maximum speed in comparison to other players? Are you able to maintain near-maximum speed repeatedly during a match?

Chapters: 8.3 & 8.4

$$\overline{20}$$

Agility   *GK – CB – FB – DM – CM – AM – F*

How quickly can you change your body position and direction while maintaining good balance?
How quick and light on your feet are you? Can you twist and turn while running with the ball
and still maintain your balance?

Chapters: 8.3 & 8.4

$$\frac{}{20}$$

Jumping   *GK – CB – FB – DM – CM – AM – F*

How high can you jump from a standing position and a running position? Are you able to
regularly outjump your opponent? How well do you time your jumps when going for a header?

Chapters: 8.2 & 8.4

$$\frac{}{20}$$

Strength   *GK – CB – FB – DM – CM – AM – F*

How strong are you compared to other players in your position? How well do you hold off
challenges from opponents?

Chapters: 8.2 & 8.4

$$\frac{}{20}$$

Stamina   *CB – FB – DM – CM – AM – F*

How good is your stamina compared to other players? Can you run as much near the end of a
match as at the beginning?

Chapters: 8.1 & 8.4

$$\frac{}{20}$$

11.5 - Off the Field

Diet   *GK – CB – FB – DM – CM – AM – F*

Do you have a healthy and balanced diet? How well do you eat before and after a match?

Chapters: 9.3

$$\frac{}{20}$$

Hydration   *GK – CB – FB – DM – CM – AM – F*

How well do you keep yourself hydrated in training and on match days? Do you drink the
correct fluids?

Chapters: 9.3

$$\frac{}{20}$$

Preparation & Injury Prevention *GK – CB – FB – DM – CM – AM – F*

Do you have a set warming-up and stretching routine? Do you perform the routine before every
training session and match? Do you have the correct equipment? E.g. Soccer cleats, shin guards.

Chapters: 9.1 & 9.2

20

Injury Recovery *GK – CB – FB – DM – CM – AM – F*

How well do you look after yourself after getting injured? Do you allow yourself time to heal
and not overexert the injured body part too quickly?

Chapters: 9.2

20

Training *GK – CB – FB – DM – CM – AM – F*

How hard do you work in training? Are you constantly trying to improve yourself?

Chapters: 10 – 10.5

20

11.6 - Set Pieces

Throw-Ins *FB – DM – CM – AM*

How accurate are your throw-Ins? How far can you throw the ball?

Chapters: 7.4

20

Free Kicks *CB – FB – DM – CM – AM – F*

How good are your shooting free kicks? How good are your crossing free kicks? Can you strike
the ball with both power and accuracy from free kicks?

Chapters: 1.2, 1.6, 1.8 & 7.1

20

Corners *CB – FB – DM – CM – AM – F*

How accurate are your corners? Can you keep the ball away from the opposing goalkeeper and
the first defender when taking a corner?

Chapters: 1.2, 1.8 & 7.2

20

Penalties *CB – FB – DM – CM – AM – F*

How good are you at taking penalties? Do you have a high goal ratio for penalties?

Chapters: 1.2 & 7.3

20

11.7 - Goalkeeper

Handling *GK*

How well can you hold the ball when attempting to catch it? If you can't catch the ball can you deflect it away from danger?

Chapters: 6.2

20

Shot Stopping *GK*

How well can you stop shots at different heights and speeds? How good is your shot stopping technique?

Chapters: 6.2

20

Reflexes *GK*

How quickly do you react to shots? Can you dive onto the ground quickly? Can you reach balls quickly that are heading for the top or bottom corner of the goal?

Chapters: 6.1

20

One-on-ones *GK*

How well can you deal with a one-on-one situation with an attacker? Can you get off your line and close down the space quickly?

Chapters: 6.2

20

Reading the Game *GK*

How well can you read and predict the game? How well can you make decisions based on your reading of the game?

Chapters: 2 – 2.8 & 6.1

20

Punching *GK*

How well do you time your punches? How good is your punching technique? How far are you able to punch the ball away from goal?

Chapters: 6.2

20

Kicking   *GK*

How good are your kicking techniques? How accurate are your kicks? How far can you kick the ball?

Chapters: 1.2 & 6.2

20

Throwing   *GK*

How good are your throwing techniques? How accurate are your throws? How far can you throw the ball?

Chapters: 6.2

20

55092403R00110

Made in the USA
Lexington, KY
10 September 2016